LIFE LESSONS FROM HIP-HOP

LIFE LESSONS FROM HIP-HOP

GRANT BRYDON

CONTENTS

FOREWORD

BY BRANDON 'JINX' JENKINS

I can't remember the exact quote, but I think podcaster Taxstone who something like, "You can raise a kid on Jadakiss lyrics." Man, I felt that shit. Growing up in New Jersey in the 1990s and 2000s, I was bombarded with heavy doses of lyric-packed raps from some of the East Coast's greatest emcees. The era was brimming with artists who wanted to make you dance but—more importantly for me—the genre was also home to self-appointed professors and autobiographers ready to share instructions to live by: The LOX, Mobb Deep, Cam'ron, Biggie, Hov—too many to name off the dome.

Even though I was often listening to music with friends, and discussing the lyrics, this relationship with the music felt singular, as if the advice was only being shared with me, from the artists I chose to listen to. My own compass.

Later, the illegal beauty of Napster proved to me that this genius lived everywhere, beyond the jurisdiction of my region and immediate taste. Getting older, more intelligent, more articulate, and more traveled, opened me up to conversations with others that revealed they too were inheriting wisdom from young men and women in the culture. And not just in the music. It was in the magazines, the radio interviews, in the liner notes of the albums. It was everywhere.

Hip-hop plays in all these spaces. It's not just a soundtrack or a groove to dance to. In its full form, it's a school of thought, damn near a religion. And its participants are both instructor and student: Clergy and congregation. It's that same beautiful dynamic that is as much utility as it is ornament. For all its desire and decoration, hip-hop is home to a growing set of schematics about how to go about (and how not to go about) this thing we call life. How to get up, get out, and get something. How to maintain your stance. How to pivot at life's most important junctures. How to look in the mirror and be cool with the person looking back.

This practice isn't strictly from the mouths of emcees when they're confined to the recording booth; it's ingrained in all of us who love this shit, at all times. We are cells constantly ricocheting our perspectives off one another in this living organism that is hip-hop.

Speaking to Grant over the years, reading his work and collaborating with him, it's clear that he's gifted. It's like he has super-human vision. No, he can't see through bank vault doors or tell you what's behind a brick wall. What I'm referring to is his ability to look beneath the surface, beyond the immediate, digging deep toward the soul of his subject—whether that be an artist's creative process, the essence and history of an underground movement, or embracing the spectrum of a person's emotional range.

As a writer—or honestly, just a person living with a smartphone—I'm sure we'd all like to believe our strength comes from our ability to produce: to move the pen, to publish, and to have something to

"IN ITS FULL FORM, [HIP-HOP IS] A SCHOOL OF THOUGHT, DAMN NEAR A RELIGION"

say, all the time. But Grant has shown, time-and-time again, that there is an immense power in listening and simply being present—especially when it comes to hip-hop culture. And he uses that superb vision of his to peer beneath the culture's top layer, zoom in, and focus on the essence. Be it in song or conversation. He sees the inherent value of the community and its most prominent minds. He knows, like I know, that if you're looking for it, hip-hop can guide your path. It can be your compass.

INTRODUCTION

I believe in hip-hop as a powerful force for personal development. Since its inception, the expression of self has been at its core. For the young Black and Latinx people in the Bronx in the '70s, hip-hop was a way to use their voices, resisting control by the system that continues to oppress them. It will always belong to these communities. As it has continued to amplify voices, its power has inspired, educated, and motivated people from every corner of the planet. Hip-hop was viral before we ever used that word to describe pop culture phenomena.

I made the pilgrimage to New York City in my late teens, where I had the privilege of hearing from pioneering MC Grandmaster Caz. He spoke about how hip-hop takes things that already exist and combines them with something to create something new: an athletic shoe with a pair of jeans, a rap verse with a soul sample or, in the early days, the electricity from a street light powering a sound system.

Hip-hop is without a doubt one of the most important art movements that the world has ever seen. But as the culture has expanded across the globe, it's transformed into something so much more—something words fail to describe. You can catch it through the way someone wears their clothes, the way they hold themselves, the way they talk, and the way they think. Hip-hop motivates those who engage with it to move forward on their quest towards self-actualisation.

Hip-hop has shaped my identity. It's been the lens through which I've engaged with the world since I was a kid. Growing up, I was obsessed with finding new artists, and then deciphering the subjects in their lyrics. This led me on a journey of discovery, into film, art, dance, sport, and popular culture. It helped me find my friends and become a part of a global community. Above all, hip-hop helped me to consider my identity, my values, and my principles, and what I want to represent during my time on Earth.

While it had served this purpose subconsciously during my adolescence, a major turning point in my life—and the first interview that appears in this book—was when I interviewed J. Cole in 2014. Driven by the "hustle hard" and "no days off" mentality of hip-hop's entrepreneurial spirit at the time, I was obsessed with productivity and career progression. I had never taken the time to consider the importance of self-care, or even the person I was outside of my work. I hadn't yet realized that I was allowing work-related anxiety to burn me out, and I was overlooking much of what I had to be thankful for. Cole's words brought me back into myself and changed the way I perceived the true wisdom that my favourite artists were imparting through their lyrics, as well as my approach to the work that I was doing as a journalist.

Shortly after this, I was given a copy of psychotherapist Richard Carlson's self-help classic *Don't Sweat the Small Stuff*. I then began to conceptualise this book, which has taken me the past eight years to refine. I hoped to create something that humanizes artists who are often drained of their personhood until they become memes and caricatures to be packaged and sold. I look to each and every person who I have had the pleasure of sharing an interview with as a mentor in their own way. These are some of the lessons I've learned from conversations with the most creative, successful, and inspiring minds of our generation. My aim is to identify teachable moments so others can hopefully experience a small part of the transformative effect that this wisdom has had on my own life.

Hip-hop is much more than a genre of music, so expect to read about people in these pages who have interacted with the culture in a broader sense, from R&B superstar Kehlani and pioneering podcaster Combat Jack, to fashion icon NIGO and New York radio-heavyweight

Ebro Darden. I've always tried to allow my curiosity to be my guide, and to stay as open-minded as possible, which has led me to interview a broad range of insightful people, and I wanted that to be reflected here.

I have chosen to use a collective "we" that unites myself and you, the reader. Of course, we are all different, and this is important to acknowledge from the outset. The lessons here are my own interpretations, and, like any interview, may not always be exactly what the artist themselves intended for me to take away from our conversations. However, they have all impacted my life in some way, and I want to acknowledge the positive impact that they have had on me.

That also means it's likely that you will read something in here that affects you in a different way than it has me. All 50 of these short features are starting points to broader conversations that you can take into your life and consider for yourself, or with people around you. Your personal interpretation is very welcome, and I hope you walk away from reading this book with some new ideas to help you on your own journey.

"HIP-HOP IS ONE OF THE MOST IMPORTANT ART MOVEMENTS THE WORLD HAS EVER SEEN"

I'm so grateful to everyone that has answered questions throughout my career. There are so many more heroes of mine and people for whom I have the utmost respect than I could possibly have fit into these pages. I thank everyone who has tried to help satisfy my curiosity, but hope that—just like Pharrell Williams—my curiosity is never satisfied.

CHAPTER ONE
MOTIVATION

DEFINE SUCCESS
J. COLE

"What does success look like to you?" I've asked hundreds of artists the same question, and the answers vary massively. The most common responses make reference to core values such as happiness and security, particularly in the context of friends and family. Interestingly, a large percentage of the responses I've received begin with a qualifying statement that success is not about money. After asking so many successful people for their definition of success, my main takeaway has been that it is different for everyone, and when setting off on a quest for self-improvement, it's worth asking: how do we achieve success if we don't yet know what it is?

J. Cole was in London a few days before the release of *2014 Forest Hills Drive*. I met up with him and he urged me to consider my own definition of success: "You're doing something you love and you're being productive in it—really getting out into the world and creating things you want to, and that's the joy right there," he said. I'd mentioned that the music I loved often celebrated monetary success, but excessive wealth didn't seem particularly realistic through my burgeoning career as a freelance music journalist.

"But by focusing on money that doesn't exist, you're not appreciating fully the blessings that you're getting from your dream," he continued. "It's pulling you away from the moment, it's steering you the wrong way."

Ahead of releasing *2014 Forest Hills Drive*, Cole returned to his hometown of Fayetteville, North Carolina, where he'd purchased the house he grew up in (which his mother had lost to repossession), and in the process had come closer to his own idea of success. This he defined at the time as "finding out what's important in life and living that everyday—or trying to."

Cole admitted that earlier in life he'd also assumed success came with a price tag. "I didn't want to worry about bills or anything financial, and I thought that would be happiness," he recalled. "I

"EVERY STEP WAS NECESSARY FOR ME TO COME TO THE UNDERSTANDING I'M AT NOW"

got to a level where I don't gotta worry about bills or anything financial and [I] was like 'Wait, I ain't happy yet?'"

The process of returning home to North Carolina, after studying in New York and relocating to Los Angeles, helped Cole gain perspective. "Now I see my whole life from an aerial point of view and I see it was absolutely necessary that I left," he explained. "It's absolutely necessary that everything that happened in my career happened; every step was necessary for me to come to the understanding I'm at now, which is way more centered around love and appreciation. [What's important to me is] a real genuine connection to people and to yourself, basically."

Each journey toward finding our personal definition of success will be unique, but that question of "what does success look like?" is a worthwhile consideration to carry with us. Like anything in life, success is a process, but we can only reach our destination if we know where we're trying to go.

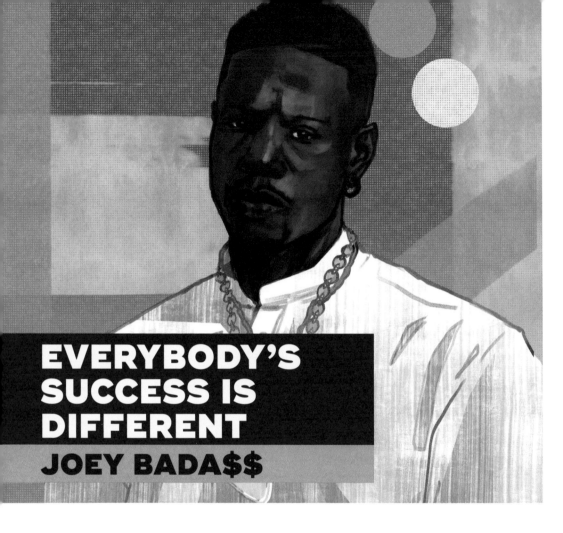

EVERYBODY'S SUCCESS IS DIFFERENT
JOEY BADA$$

It's vital to ensure that the success we're working toward is our own. It is unlikely that we will feel fulfilled by creating a copycat version of someone else's vision. Success isn't one size fits all, and just as nobody's definition is the same, neither are the journeys that help us to get there.

Although it can sometimes be tempting to replicate steps that have been fruitful for others, Joey Bada$$ told me he's learned that everyone's success is different.

Joey believes that this is even more difficult to realize in the age of social media, where much of our time is spent observing and consuming the highlights of other people's lives. "When you're exposed to so much externally, it's hard not to compare or measure yourself against what you're seeing going on around you," he explained.

It's helpful to separate ourselves from what we see others doing, whether they're celebrating career milestones, or relationship goals, or attending events we aren't at. Evaluating our own lives and experiences by comparison is not helpful, and furthermore it can also lead us to be resentful and jealous, rather than celebratory of other people's wins. By separating our own success from that of our peers, we're able to feel joy for other people's achievements without judging ourselves against them.

"At the end of the day, there's always going to be someone who is more advanced than you, or further in life than you are," Joey accepted. "But that is no reason to measure up your own life or your own success because everyone's path is different."

Of course, once we begin to experience a level of success, it's natural for our understanding of success to expand and evolve. After blowing up in his teens with his *1999* mixtape—which was more reminiscent of classic Golden Age hip-hop than on trend with the contemporary sounds of the time—Joey continued to build his career as a rapper by staying true to his own vision. While he's continued to hit new milestones in music, he has simultaneously been developing a career as an actor, recently winning an Oscar for his starring role in the short movie *Two Distant Strangers*.

Had Joey been following someone else's blueprint too closely, he might have missed that fork in the road which led him into a whole new career path. "It could be easy to miss or overlook your own opportunities if you're caught up on what's going on with somebody else," said Joey. "My formula is not going to work for everyone. And it's the same thing with your formula."

Now, a decade since *1999* dropped, Joey is as proud of the timeless cult classic as he was when he released it—a testament to the way he's traveled unfalteringly along his own path since the very beginning. The key, Joey said, is to never lose sight of what is motivating you at the beginning of your journey, before there were comparisons to any external factors: "You can never make it more about wanting to be successful than it is about wanting to do what it is you do."

While it's good to be inspired by those around us, the more deeply we internalize factors from the outside—often by comparing ourselves to others—the more we will struggle with finding the success that is truly our own. If we can filter thoughts and ideas through our own personal values and beliefs as much as possible, we will be much more resilient in reaching our own definition of success.

COMMIT TO INSPIRATION

FLO MILLI

Inspiration is all around us. We can find it everywhere. But in order for it to have an impact, we need to actively engage with it. We need to make a commitment. This can be something that seems relatively simple in the moment, but can quickly be amplified. That droplet of an idea we could have so easily allowed to float by can become a pivotal moment in the trajectory of our lives. Flo Milli committed to finding inspiration through the seemingly minor act of buying a notebook.

Flo's grandmother had always told her to dream big, and one day when she arrived home from school and turned on the TV she was hit with the stimulus that would spark a new obsession. As had become routine, she tuned in to the BET channel just in time for the iconic music video show *106 & Park*. It was October 2010 and Nicki Minaj was on the show promoting her debut album *Pink Friday*.

"I was just amazed by how much fun she was having," Flo recalled. "And I wanted to do shit that I could have fun doing and make money. So when

I saw that I was just like, 'I wanna try this shit.'"

That's when Flo decided to act on that feeling of inspiration: "I started buying notebooks from Walmart and I used to write songs in them. And I went to school rapping: I would rap for my class, rap for my best friend and her mom—they used to always tell me I was gonna be famous. It was just me falling in love with it for real."

> ## "THEY USED TO ALWAYS TELL ME I WAS GONNA BE FAMOUS"

Flo started a group called Pink Mafia with some friends and together they'd write songs which they kept in a ring binder. They would perform the songs at talent shows and her friend's parents' restaurant, but by the age of fifteen the rest of the girls weren't

interested in rapping. But Flo remained committed. "A year later, I started going to the studio and actually rapping," she said. "That's when Flo Milli came about."

Making a commitment to the inspiration that struck her that evening has paid off. As one of the most exciting rappers of her generation, Flo Milli stands out by sticking to a music-making approach that was born from watching *106 & Park* and writing in her notebooks. "She has a bit of an old-school approach, as far as lyrics go," her A&R, Skane Dolla, told me. "That's what attracted me to her. She's lyrical with the punchlines and that's my era of hip-hop."

When you're hit with inspiration, it's important to act on it. No matter how insignificant it may seem, try to make a commitment to follow up on these moments of creative revelation. Explore possibilities and avoid putting obstacles in your way: you never know how far an idea could take you.

**IT DOESN'T
TAKE MUCH**

LIL PEEP

It's easy to feel like we need more than we have in order to create. But some of the most innovative artists have been able to change the landscape of music with surprisingly little.

I interviewed Lil Peep one morning while he wandered around the parking lot of the Anaheim Angels stadium, waiting to play Day N Night Fest, two months before the tragic events that would take his life much too soon. He'd recently released his *Come Over When You're Sober, Pt.1* mixtape, which introduced legions of new fans to his boundary-blurring sound.

During our conversation he talked about the beginning of his journey in music-making, which began as an escape from depression. "I did what everyone else who inspired me in the underground did. You run into the Guitar Center, spend $300, and then the whole world is in your hands," he explained. "Literally you just need to put in the hard work at that point. It doesn't take much, it doesn't take an insane recording studio. All of my biggest songs were made in my bedroom on a $200 microphone."

Peep became one of the pioneering forces behind the fusion of emo melodies and trap rhythm that has continued to become increasingly prevalent in mainstream music. He made a huge impact on music in his short career, and

"ALL OF MY BIGGEST SONGS WERE MADE IN MY BEDROOM ON A $200 MICROPHONE"

did so by using his creativity to maximize what was available to him. The driving force behind Peep's music was how he fused his influences in a way that was authentic to him, and this happened without the need for expensive studio equipment.

Sometimes we can put off our ambitions, placing invisible barriers in our own path, such as the excuse that we need something that isn't available to us. Often this is just a defence mechanism which we're using to mask the fear that comes with pushing off from the starting line. There is usually a creative solution we can find to work around whatever we think we're missing, and finding this can be an adventure that leads to something pioneering and innovative.

BE A LEADER
KAASH PAIGE

In a world that's obsessed with followers, it can be more efficient to hop onto the latest trend in pursuit of overnight success than to stand up and contribute our own thoughts and ideas. There's nothing wrong with liking what is popular, but if we continue to blindly follow and never form our own opinions and identities, it's unlikely that we'll end up feeling creatively, emotionally, or intellectually fulfilled.

During her senior year at high school, Kaash Paige made the decision to become a leader. She told me that throughout school she'd been content as a follower and had struggled to find her own voice or opinion. "Being in high school, you're around all of these different egos, these different opinions, that you get lost," she explained.

Eventually Kaash decided to challenge herself. "I jumped off the porch and was like 'I want to be the artist that everyone's listening to,'" she recalled. She wanted her peers to be asking each other, "Have you heard that new Kaash Paige?", the same way they would about Drake's new releases.

There were a lot of kids rapping at Kaash's school, so tapping into her newly adopted leader mentality, she realized that taking an alternative approach would help her to stand out. She decided to lean further into singing than rapping, recording a track called "Dnd" over an instrumental by producer Dream Koala who she found on YouTube. Her instinct was correct, and the new melodic approach cut through the music that her peers were making. Soon enough "Dnd" became popular at school. The song's success far exceeded Kaash's expectations, and two years later a rerecorded version called "Love Songs" would become a viral hit, leading her to a deal with the iconic Def Jam Recordings.

Leadership does leave you vulnerable to criticism, which is perhaps the reason many people would prefer to remain a follower. Kaash has learned to accept that with everything she does, there will be people who talk negatively about it. "If you choose to live this lifestyle, you're going to get talked about regardless, but anybody is gonna get talked about to the day they die," she explained. "That's just life in general."

Kaash tries not to concern herself with criticism—in fact, she has "overthinking kills" tattooed on her neck as a note-to-self—but when she does catch herself overthinking, she protects her confidence by reminding herself that all of the artists she loves the most go through the same thing. "I just like to always keep myself motivated and confident, because I never had that growing up," she said. "I always was super down on myself, never had any confidence. So now that I actually have that confidence, I just always try to stay happy and just try to keep growing."

There is great value in allowing ourselves the space to stand out by considering what we really feel, what we agree or disagree with, what we like or dislike, so that we can be authentic to who we really are. We can only be content fitting in for so long—eventually we need to step out and be true to ourselves if we're to live a full life.

CHAPTER TWO
CREATIVITY

EMBRACE YOUR INFLUENCES
TRAVIS SCOTT

We're all a patchwork of different influences that we pick up throughout our lives: where we're from, who we grew up around, the music we listen to, the movies we watch, and our personal history. Each layer of our experience and taste adds uniqueness to our way of being. Originality lies in embracing the range of influences that impact each of us in a distinctive way.

Growing up in Houston, Travis Scott was immersed in a culture where larger-than-life local heroes instilled him with hometown pride. He looked up to the swagger of artists like Lil' Flip and Paul Wall, and the non-conformity of the Rap-A-Lot Records movement. "Every artist on that label was a major inspiration," he told me, as he prepared to play his first London show in 2014. "They invented that whole independence of just doing your thing and not worrying about nobody."

While continuing in their lineage, Travis has added further layers to his own portrait of the city. The candy paint and syrupy soul of DJ Screw are present, but so too is the visual language of directors like Robert Rodriguez and Quentin Tarantino and their depictions of the South. Travis's musical taste sees him inviting alternative acts such as James Blake, M.I.A, Bon Iver, Toro y Moi, and Tame Impala to add a sense of eclecticism to his ever-expanding sonic world. It's unsurprising that his biggest personal inspiration is Kid Cudi—who's real name Scott Mescudi, inspired Travis's stage name. Kid Cudi is known for a similarly heterogeneous approach. "He's so ill because he can body n****s like a Jeezy, but still cut through like Twigs or MGMT," Travis enthused.

I interviewed Travis again in 2017, but this time we were in Houston where he was working on his psychedelic epic *Astroworld*. The album draws its inspiration from a theme park that closed down while he was a teenager. "It got taken away from the city, which is like taking our heart out," he said, during a late-night drive. "It was a monument for us kids and our ideas." He has fond memories of attending the park on

"EVERY ARTIST ON [RAP-A-LOT RECORDS] WAS A MAJOR INSPIRATION"

Halloween for Fright Fest and spending summer days there riding roller coasters like Greezed Lightnin'. The richness of inspiration that Travis drew from these coming-of-age experiences oozes throughout the record.

It is vital, as human beings, that we embrace what motivates us, changes our perspective, and gives us new ideas. We can freely explore the things that we're passionate about; enthusiasm is infectious. Our influences make us who we are and can't be overlooked, no matter how small their impact may seem. Even if at times it feels like we're being derivative, pulling in our individual set of experiences and interests will help us to center ourselves and create something authentic and original.

CREATE FEELINGS
070 SHAKE

People often talk about creating memories, but perhaps it is even more important to retain the feelings attached to those memories. We rarely remember full events from our past, but we can generally recall the emotion that we were experiencing at the time.

In the way that an old photograph can unearth a buried memory, 070 Shake aims to create music that evokes feelings which listeners can return to repeatedly.

A few weeks before she released her debut album *Modus Vivendi* on Kanye West's G.O.O.D Music label, we sat down for an interview in a quiet bar on the outskirts of Williamsburg. Shake expressed that she experiences a rollercoaster of anxiety, nervousness, and excitement ahead of a release, but this is all outweighed by what she manages to translate to others once the music reaches her listeners.

"You could kind of [see the feelings] in people's faces and their body and their body language. You see when they feel something and it's so different," she explained of her live shows. "That's why I

do this shit, it's to see people feel. That's why performance is my favorite part of it, because I can actually firsthand see how this is making you feel."

Shake believes that feeling is the key to creating memories. "There's so many things in life I feel like I don't remember because I didn't really stop at that moment and feel something for it," she admitted. "So when you think about a significant other that you've had, you remember that feeling that they gave you. That's all you really remember; you felt something that you carried on with you."

Shake understands this alchemy— music transforming into emotion—because she's felt it first hand, through artists like Michael Jackson, Kanye West, Kid Cudi, The Weeknd, and Queen. "I want to give people that feeling, because I think that's what's carried on," she said. "The songs you remember now are songs that said something, because you translate this feeling through words and rhythm."

As a result, Shake's work doesn't conform to a lot of the traditional rules of

"I WANT TO GIVE PEOPLE THAT FEELING, BECAUSE I THINK THAT'S WHAT'S CARRIED ON"

music-making or genre. With emotion at the forefront, she'll pull from a toolkit of words, vocal approaches, production techniques, and instrumentals, selecting the elements that are best suited to painting the emotion she wants to convey.

It's vital that we don't lose emotion to the rigorousness of our creative process. At the core of all of our creation, and shared human experience in general, is feeling. To truly connect with others, that will always be our driving force.

DON'T OVER
THINK SHIT

KENNY BEATS

Overthinking can strip a great idea of its essence, or worse, stop it from being realized altogether. It's something that all artists have dealt with at some point, so much so that producer Kenny Beats has a neon sign in his recording booth, reminding his collaborators: "Don't Over Think Shit".

"There's never been a person who's walked in there and been like 'Turn that off,'" he told me. "Everyone sees it like, 'I could use that.' And, honestly, the reason I put it in there is because I overthink absolutely everything."

Initially, the phrase became Kenny's mantra during a phone call with his manager, and it's become a source of comfort in the studio for the extended family of rappers and vocalists that he works with. "When an artist comes in and maybe they're struggling with a lyric, or maybe they're doubting themselves, and the only thing they have to look at is the microphone and a giant sign that says Don't Over Think Shit—it tends to point them in the right direction."

While working with Denzel Curry on their collaborative project UNLOCKED, Kenny made the realization that overthinking can potentially cause work to lose its originality.

"I was listening to so much Madlib," he explained. "I found the imperfection and the record skips and the odd meters and the unusual tempos and the records to be my biggest influences ever."

With UNLOCKED, he and Denzel—another self-proclaimed overthinker—had the space to break the rules and experiment, refreshing their excitement about their respective creative practices: "We started really trusting each other," Kenny reflected. "Every little bit of our personality that we throw into here that's random or off-kilter or unusual: that's what makes this project this project."

There are many situations in life that would be made far easier if we were to have a neon sign in sight, reminding us not to overthink. Our gut reaction is a very valuable one, formed from all of the experiences that have led us to where we are, and we can put our trust in that. When talking about creative work in particular, it's advisable not to allow thinking to get in the way of what we're trying to bring to fruition. It's fine to edit later, but without getting that initial raw idea out—warts and all—we could potentially miss out on making something great.

DON'T BE AFRAID TO START OVER

BROCKHAMPTON

While working on a creative project it's common to hit a wall and get stuck. Sometimes, no matter what we do to try and get it back on track, we just can't keep things flowing: we struggle to find the excitement that was there at the beginning, and it feels like we're floundering, and making no progress. When we find ourselves feeling this way we mustn't be afraid to start over again.

The effort we've already put in won't go to waste. We may return to the project at another time, when we've gathered more information, inspiration, or perspective. An element of the work might even find its way into another project. But the work in progress will always be there, just as we left it. It's never a failure to go back to the beginning.

BROCKHAMPTON scrapped three albums before they managed to make their 2018 album *iridescence*.

The collective had accelerated to prominence the previous year with their *SATURATION* trilogy, releasing all three entries across a six-month period. But when it came to following up that incredibly prolific run, they found themselves struggling.

"It felt like a disaster, and our worlds were crumbling," JOBA told me. "But when I listen back to the songs that we made, a month and a half ago, I feel like I've grown and I hear growth in everyone else."

While it was tough to experience at the time, the process was not without value. "When you care about something, you'll know that it's not right," said Kevin Abstract (pictured). "Sometimes it's better to start over... Making three albums this year and scrapping them, then making this one has been like therapy; learning more things about

myself and becoming more confident with my work—trying to get back to the root of why I do this, which is because there's something in me that feels like I need to make music."

Perhaps one of the biggest obstacles was BROCKHAMPTON's own success, which led to a huge change of circumstance and required time for the group to process. "Being an artist is easy, you're just painting. But being an artist with success, that's when it gets hard," Kevin explained. "How are you going to sell that painting, or what if people don't like the painting? Then you have to make a decision at that point: 'Do I give a fuck what people think or do I just want to paint?' [Making this album] feels like painting again."

Not every stage of the creative process needs to lead to a final product. In fact, the pressure of making a final product can get in the way of important work. Moments of experimentation, even ones that don't quite work out, nonetheless teach us something about ourselves. It's often as valuable to understand why something isn't right for us than why something is. That is information we'll carry with us, even if it's in our subconscious, into future situations. We need never be afraid to start over. Works in progress always have value.

> **"WHEN YOU CARE ABOUT SOMETHING, YOU'LL KNOW THAT IT'S NOT RIGHT"**

DON'T LOSE THE CONNECTION

EBRO DARDEN

While making something, we're often driven by our own natural impulses. But our creative progression is enriched if we understand the deeper context of the work we're doing.

HOT 97 and Apple Music 1 radio personality Ebro Darden believes it's his responsibility to help his listeners understand how their favorite new music fits into a wider cultural context.

Ebro's own broad taste in music came through the lens of the hip-hop that he listened to in his youth, which introduced him to a rich tapestry of other genres.

"Jungle Brothers and Queen Latifah made house records. Sugarhill rhymed over disco records," he told me. "Then when you get to the '90s, what they call the golden era of hip-hop, they were sampling jazz records and funk records, all these different genres of music. The Beastie Boys sampled rock records. Run-DMC sampled rock records."

Wherever possible, Ebro tries to utilize his time on air to champion what he calls a "second tier of discovery":

introducing his listeners to the moments that paved the way for the new music they love. "[A new] album comes out and you're like 'Oh, shit, I love this album,'" he explained. "You don't naturally go: 'This album was made possible because this, this, this, and this already happened.'" He believes that it's important to retain a connection to the wider context. "I find myself not only finding what is influencing artists that are making music right now, but taking them one step back to the things that influenced the artists that are influencing them, so that we don't lose that connection musically. I think that's important," he said.

Without a connection to history and context, by paying attention to that second tier of discovery, so much pioneering music would never have been made. For the advancement of music and the generation of new ideas, it's important for people to engage in a larger way than exclusively focusing on current trends.

Even if we're not directly drawing on their influence, it's always valuable to understand where our creative work engages with ideas and themes explored by artists that came before us. While this could easily become an overwhelming task, a good starting point is to look at that second tier: who inspired those that have motivated us? How does our work relate to or engage with those that came before us? Considering questions like these will help us to understand the mark that we're making on the world around us, and how we're connecting to a community of like-minded creatives, beyond the confines of time and space. Such powerful discoveries can provide clarity around our creative purpose and help to trigger further inspirational impulses that help our work to keep progressing.

ALLOW IDEAS TO POLLINATE
CAM'RON

When sharing ideas, we can easily become attached to the initial reaction. If we're met with negativity, that may bring a premature end to our line of thinking. Equally, an overly positive reaction can make us hurry or become complacent, risk averse, or clouded by unrealistically high expectations. Often we actually need to give our ideas time to settle, to grow with others, and spread away from us. No matter how our ideas are received, it's helpful to stay balanced until we get a lay of the land.

Cam'ron cultivated a movement around himself and his crew, Dipset, that spread from Harlem to the world and has endured for generations. After building a modest following in the late '90s he took his career to the next level in the early 2000s when he signed with the iconic Roc-A-Fella Records, flooding the streets with mixtapes and dominating hip-hop radio.

Despite Dipset's dominance across the global hip-hop community, through mixtapes, specialist radio, and clubs, many casual music fans at the time would have likely been aware of only a few tracks that crossed over to the mainstream. But the crew continued to cultivate their movement with a cult fanbase that continues to support them over 20 years later. "We only really had two big commercial records," Cam'ron told me, recalling that early period. "Though we had great records in the club and [were successful] underground. As far as Top 40 hits, we only had two or three of those. And I think that kind of helped us, because pop fans aren't loyal. So, if you come out in the beginning, sell four or five million, and a lot of it is to the pop audience, you never build your fanbase. I think that's what we did and why we are still successful today."

Through their core fans following them from the ground up, Cam, Juelz Santana, Jim Jones, and Freekey Zekey resonate deeply with a generation of rap fans, and their legacy has continued to extend through online communities.

Iconic imagery from that era—in particular Cam's unforgettable baby-pink fur look at the 2002 New York Fashion Week, complete with a matching pink flip phone —has become prevalent once again, and online creators across music, fashion, and pop culture have paid tribute to Dipset with everything from socks to duvets.

"Basically I never tried to do what anybody else did. That wasn't purposely, it's just me being myself," Cam reflected. "I didn't realize it, but the Internet is starting to show me that all the stuff that I've done in the past, how people are showing love for it. Because you do a lot of stuff—back when I started—and you're not sure if people like it or not. But now you go on Instagram, you got people with Cam'ron dresses, Cam'ron candles, Cam'ron watches, Cam'ron coffee cups. It feels good to be appreciated and just know that me being different is still relevant."

A good idea can stand the test of time, but implementing one effectively requires resilience and careful analysis. We can't be put off easily: if we really believe in something, it's more than likely that others will too. We need to stay committed to the process, allow our ideas to germinate through ourselves and others who believe in it, and watch them start to pollinate it in their own ways.

CHAPTER THREE
AUTHENTICITY

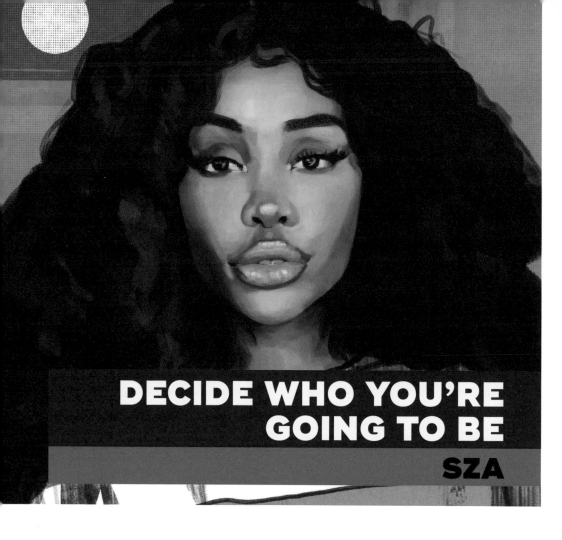

DECIDE WHO YOU'RE GOING TO BE

SZA

Although there is a lot that we can't change about the situation we're born into, and who we are as a result, it's imperative that we remember we do have a lot of say in the type of person we want to be. We don't have to limit ourselves by accepting the path that others have taken, and we can make choices about who we are and who we might become in the future.

I interviewed SZA on the theme of "the American Dream" in 2014. She had recently signed with Top Dawg Entertainment and just released her Z EP. "I'm Muslim and I'm Black, so the American Dream isn't something that was ever possible for me," said SZA.

"Especially as a kid, you don't grow up being like 'Yeah, everything is possible.'"

SZA told me that instead she'd had to make a choice to actively embody the things that she wanted to stand for. "I think at some point you just have to decide who you're gonna be and how you're gonna get there, and then no one is going to stop you," she said.

Of course, this doesn't mean that there won't be challenges, and that we won't have to adapt our plan as we go along in order to tackle the obstacles that stand in our way. But SZA has very much embodied these words as she has gone on to become one of the most important voices of this generation.

By embracing her sense of self, SZA has followed a path of her own making, recording the classic album *Ctrl* a few years later, tapping into her psyche, and being vulnerable in a way that few will ever dare to be. Despite growing up with the odds stacked against her, she has used her power to be a force for positivity that has impacted fans all over the world and established herself as a singular talent who will be remembered throughout history.

Society often tries to push us to conform, to play our role and follow a path that is laid out for us, and often it can seem like there is very little we can do about it. However, we must be empowered by the fact that whatever

> ## "DECIDE WHO YOU'RE GONNA BE AND HOW YOU'RE GONNA GET THERE, AND THEN NO ONE IS GOING TO STOP YOU"

challenges we face in life, there is always a choice in how we navigate them. Even if at the back of our heads a voice tells us we are unworthy, we must remind ourselves that we are deserving of self-actualization. Deciding who we want to be isn't about rejecting who we are right now; it's about embracing that, making choices, and taking control of how we can use the self as a force for good, to help make positive change and uplift those who find themselves in our orbit.

GET COMFORTABLE IN YOUR OWN SKIN

J.I.D

When we take too much on board from those around us, we can find ourselves being knocked off course; relying on the opinions of others or adopting too much of the style and characteristics of those who we look up to. But to live in a fulfilling way, it's important that we're able to accept, embrace, and find comfort in who we are. We need to be able to evaluate situations and make decisions for ourselves. This isn't something that will happen overnight, and it's likely to be an ongoing process that will continue throughout our lives.

Through his studio practice, J.I.D has learned to avoid the opinions of others until he's finished with a piece of work. Once he has completed an idea by following his own instincts, he can present the work to his peers. "Sometimes when I'm creating, I don't want nobody around me," he explained. "I just don't want to think about somebody else's opinion on it. Let me get through it. Let me get to the end. 'Cause you can get a lot of opinions and it can throw you off."

> ## "YOU CAN GET A LOT OF OPINIONS AND IT CAN THROW YOU OFF"

Hearing the wrong feedback during the often delicate process of creating can set him back for days. "I might think about what somebody said to me for the next three days. It might just fuck me up, because I overthink and second-guess myself a lot," he admitted. "But usually, if I'm doing it by myself and I just get the finished product, I feel like they love it every time."

Finding the confidence to create alone, and not to rely on the support of others, helped J.I.D to tell his story in a more candid way and stay true to himself. It's something that he had to work on, but it's an essential part of his artistic success. "It takes living and getting comfortable in your [own] skin," he said. "A lot of people are not

comfortable when they wake up and look in the mirror. That shit takes time, 'cause people will battle, like, 'Am I not fitting up to these standards?' But as you get older, you're like, 'Fuck that shit. Fuck what everybody else thinks.'"

While it can be helpful to ask others for feedback, it's important that we don't come to rely on this too heavily, or to seek reassurance from others. Constructive feedback is valuable, but in order for it to be used effectively we must know ourselves and be comfortable with who we are. We need to be able to live and work congruently with our core values and principles. That authenticity will help us reduce the worry and doubt that shrouds our daily lives and leads to the build up of anxiety. Developing processes that help us to have more control over our own decisions and ideas will help us to gain confidence and feel more content in our work and lives.

DON'T LOOK FOR VALIDATION
KARI FAUX

While society might make "cool" feel like it has some kind of shared definition, it's helpful to remember that it doesn't. Cool is to be defined by each of us individually. Looking to others for clarity on what we "should" like or dislike will only leave us feeling anxious and reduce our sense of autonomy.

Throughout her life, Kari Faux has learned that it's a waste of our time looking for validation from other people. "I was always kind of strange. I was that person that had different interests from my peers," she explained to me, of her childhood. "And so I just always remember talking about those things I was interested in to my peers and them looking at me with a question mark." She remembered being obsessed with Cartoon Network's Toonami programming, where she'd keep up with shows like *Dragon Ball Z*, and she loved watching WWE: "Being a little Black girl from Arkansas, who are you bonding with over wrestling and anime? So it was just one of those things where I'm not gonna not like what I like because I don't have anybody to necessarily connect with."

"YOU JUST HAVE TO KNOW THAT YOU'RE COOL"

Luckily, Kari wasn't dissuaded by the attitudes of those around her and stuck with her interests. "As I got older, I just realized, there's nothing wrong with me liking the things that I like," she recalled. "And there's nothing wrong with me wanting to share my excitement for those things that I like." She experienced feelings of embarrassment when her enthusiasm wasn't reciprocated, but that didn't change how she felt inside. "I personally have always felt like I was cool," she asserted. "You just have to know that you're cool."

By staying attuned to her own compass of cool, Kari has deepened her connection with those individuals who

engage with her creative work. "I don't think that I make anything for the average person," she said. "Anything I make is very niche and I'm aware of it." Rather than casting her net wide, she makes work that speaks to like-minded thinkers who share a similarly unique spirit and sense of self, including fellow boundary-breaking multi-hyphenates like regular collaborators Issa Rae and Donald Glover.

From her experience Kari has come to understand the concept of cool as individual, not something that can be imposed on us by others. "The only way to be uncool in my eyes is if what you're doing isn't rooted in authenticity," she explained. "There might be some things I don't care for, but that doesn't mean it's not cool to somebody else. I've just always done whatever I wanted to do, because I know for me it's more about how I feel at the end of the day and less about trying to appease people. There has to be some kind of internal desire to be happy doing what you're doing."

We have to trust our feelings about the things we value in life. If it's something that excites and motivates us, something we care about, then we can confidently define it as cool. Looking to other people for validation will only come between us and the things we want, which is not helpful. We can't waste time trying to justify our interests: the joy they contribute to our lives is more than enough.

EMBRACE WHAT MAKES YOU DIFFERENT
WIKI

No two human beings are the same. We all have our own experience of humanity. To be open to difference helps us to relate to others and move forward harmoniously with the rest of humanity. But that also means embracing and understanding the layers that separate us from our immediate peers, including our insecurities and vulnerabilities.

As the son of a Puerto Rican father and Irish-American mother, Wiki says that he struggled to understand where he was supposed to fit in when he was younger. Writing raps provided him with an outlet to explore his own identity.

"Being an MC, there's that whole idea of putting yourself on in your music, and it really being this personal, specific thing. The songs are about your shit," he told me one afternoon during an afternoon walk through Manhattan. At first, a lot of Wiki's material was self-deprecating, reflecting how he felt as he came to terms with who he is. But through writing about himself and expressing how he felt in front of global audiences, he began to develop confidence in himself. "There's always insecurities," he said. "But you're able to write about it and flip it." He came up with the "Wiki Flag"—referenced on most of his album covers—by combining the design of the Puerto Rican flag with the Irish colors of green and orange, creating a symbol to represent his heritage.

Hip-hop has a long history of turning differences into superpowers. Wiki highlights how RZA embraced his childhood obsession with Shaolin kung fu movies, lacing sound bites and references throughout the Wu-Tang Clan records to build an immersive sonic world that captured the imaginations of people all over the world. "You look at Ol' Dirty Bastard," added Wiki. "That's someone who's using the weird elements of who he is and he's making it a style and doing it with confidence... it's genuine and authentic."

These flourishes of uniqueness and specificity lead to the almost indescribable feeling that we get from experiencing truly original work. "It's a little bit of magic in the world," explained

Wiki. "It's where the fantasy and reality get to meet, because you're making it a reality and it comes from real shit." While Wiki's raps come from his lived experience, the way he presents it—the way he uses his voice, his choice of words, and beat selection—provides opportunities to embrace the quirks that make him one of a kind.

"That's such an important part of hip-hop," he said. "I think it's about being you: unapologetically and authentically you, but with flavor. And I think that's important in general. I think that spirit applies to anything."

Rather than minimizing the elements of us that may make us seem like oddballs to our friends, it's ultimately a more positive experience to embrace the things that make us *us*—even if at first that might be challenging. To be truly authentic to ourselves, we must celebrate the things that make *us* different and turn them into our superpowers.

CHAPTER FOUR

REINVENTION

REINVENT YOURSELF
MAC MILLER

Reinvention is a key part of living a creative life. While change can be scary, if we attempt to stay in our comfort zone by holding onto what is familiar to us, things will quickly become boring and we won't make meaningful progress. Each one of us is made up of so many layers, that to enjoy the fullest experience we must embrace the various aspects of our personality, even if these can seem contradictory at times.

While Mac Miller lived a tragically short life, it struck me, over the course of several interviews, how fully he allowed himself to experience the worlds he was building with each project. Even when I caught Mac after a full day of press, he'd be full of enthusiasm as we talked about the things he'd been working on.

I believe one of the factors that was intrinsic to this feeling of excitement was that Mac had the courage to experiment. On every album or mixtape he was trying something new, whether this was a different genre of music, a fresh perspective, or the invention of a new character. Drawing inspiration from underground legends like Madlib and MF DOOM, he created new personas, such as beat maker Larry Fisherman, horrorcore rapper Delusional Thomas, and jazz band Larry Lovestein & The Velvet Revival. "This month I'm in this world, next month I'm in another," he told me in 2014, just after the release of his *Faces* mixtape. Mac was unafraid to reinvent himself and this contributed to his creative evolution.

"THIS MONTH I'M IN THIS WORLD, NEXT MONTH I'M IN ANOTHER"

"I don't like sticking to a formula when it comes to making music," Mac told me in a 2016 interview around the release of his neo-soul-tinged fourth album, *The Divine Feminine*. "I'm discovering new stuff about myself every day, so it's important not to get comfortable. No one can guess what a new Mac Miller album will sound like because they all represent different parts of my life." He continued to surprise fans, transitioning from mostly rap into song for the last album he released before he passed away in 2018, *Swimming*, and its posthumous counterpart, *Circles*, in 2020.

Perhaps the most practical advice Mac left me was given in that same interview, the last we would do together. While rap is generally delivered in the first person, he'd started to search externally in order to write more broadly. "I think it helps to get outside of yourself when you are working on a record. To use your emotion and create, rather than getting locked into yourself. One thing I'm learning more and more is how to get a little more outside of myself with writing. I'm inspired by the world around me, rather than only dealing with my personal narrative."

When we feel as though we're getting a little stuck in our ways, or our excitement about the things we're investing our time in begins to falter, it's great to consider some alternative viewpoints. Bringing a fresh perspective—even if it's an imagined one—to something that we've already become very familiar with is the first step toward our next reinvention.

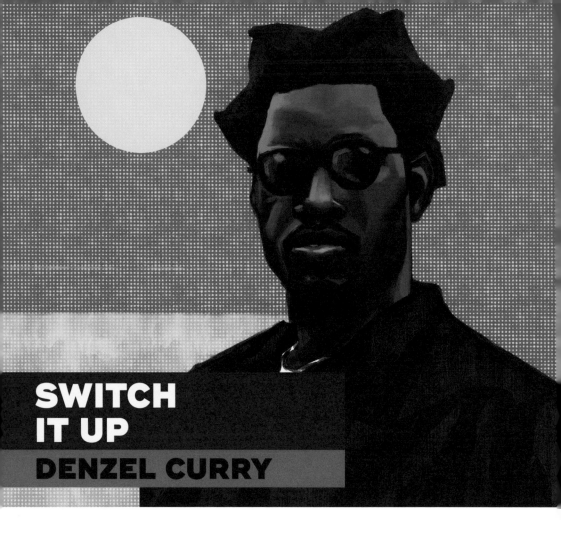

SWITCH IT UP
DENZEL CURRY

Sometimes as creatives or artists we can concern ourselves with building a catalog of work that feels, looks, or sounds like us. We want some kind of thread that runs through everything. But that can easily lead us to playing it safe. Often when we create two things that might seem very different to us, we overlook the fact that they're intrinsically bound by the fact that they all come from the same creator and draw on the same set of values and experiences. To someone else, the link between these seemingly opposing things may seem very clear.

Denzel Curry has never been afraid to create in different styles. He emerged as a pioneer of the lo-fi

Soundcloud rap wave with "Threatz" in 2013, had a viral hit single with the bottle-flip soundtrack "Ultimate" in 2015, created a critically acclaimed tribute to Miami with his fourth studio album *Zuu*, collaborated with Kenny Beats to pay homage to underground rap heroes with their *UNLOCKED* EP, and moved toward live instrumentation and introspection for *Melt My Eyez See Your Future* in 2022.

Denzel said that he'd noticed artists limiting themselves by creating the same content over and over again, and identified the way that fans became bored of knowing what to expect. "I'm not gonna be that person," he stated. "I already know how I am, I fixate myself on certain sounds. If I just keep trying to do that over time it's just gonna get watered down each time. So I try to figure out a way to change it, switch it, and do another thing."

Denzel cited the likes of Michael Jackson and André 3000 as examples of artists who have regularly surprised people by not giving them what they expected. "Even Jay-Z may keep the same rap style, but he changed up what he's doing and incorporated new elements," he said. "He did songs with Linkin Park and he didn't have to be a rocker or nothing like that, he just kept doing Jay-Z but he just chose different production because he's a great artist overall. I feel like as a great artist you've got to switch it up every time."

While it's impossible to expect what a new release by Denzel will sound like, all of the music that he's released feels organic to its creator. Each new direction is initially surprising, but it makes sense thanks to his personal commitment to it all. "You're not going to predict what my next move is going to be," he said. "I just know whatever direction I'm going to go in, I'm going to play that part, but I'mma play it seriously."

For Denzel, the aim is to keep adding value to his catalog by creating fresh and lasting work: "I want my own discography to be remembered like a Kanye West discography, or an OutKast discography, or Kendrick Lamar. Those are the only people I know with bodies of work that have stood the test of time and each record got better and better."

It's important to create each new work freely, without worrying about how it fits with the previous things we have made. Only once we have a set of several things—all creations of our own unique minds and perspectives, each created with their own identity and purpose—will the threads begin to emerge that bind them together. At that point, we'll have a much richer catalog that demonstrates who we are from different perspectives and showcases the personal growth of our creative journey.

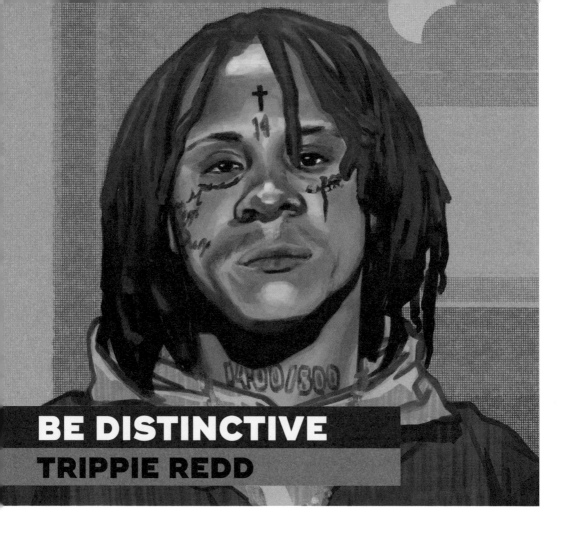

BE DISTINCTIVE
TRIPPIE REDD

We don't need to be afraid of standing out. It's important to embrace our uniqueness, as this will help us to feel congruent with the world around us—rather than trying to push things to the side or suppress thoughts and ideas because we're worried that they won't be accepted.

Trippie Redd has made a career out of being distinctive.

The Simpsons creator, Matt Groening, has been quoted as saying that the secret of designing successful cartoon characters is to create ones that are "distinct and identifiable in silhouette." The wisdom of this quote extends to anyone or anything that stands out, and this is certainly true of Trippie, who has drawn on influences from anime and video games to make himself instantly recognizable. "I do everything distinct to myself," he told me, during his first trip to London where, despite being a relatively new artist, he was already being spotted by fans, thanks to his idiosyncratic appearance. "You know me from far away, up close—two miles down the street, you gonna know it's me."

This individuality extends to Trippie's music, which exists in a sonic world of its own. While many of his peers define themselves with a particular vocal style or production choices, Trippie's most distinctive factor is his voice, which he pushes to its limits.

> ## "YOU KNOW ME FROM FAR AWAY, UP CLOSE—TWO MILES DOWN THE STREET, YOU GONNA KNOW ITS ME"

Initially, Trippie developed his experimental style in private, away from the pressure to conform: "I used to record myself a lot," he recalled. "I would just go in the booth and sing a couple melodies, play the beat, sing over the beat, overpower my voice, and all that shit.

I really lay some down that I wouldn't say around others. You know, this shit is art. I gotta work on my craft by myself sometimes."

Although Trippie admits that not all of these experiments made it out of the studio, the ones that did began to build his reputation as a truly innovative artist, whose vocal approaches range from traditional East Coast rapping to metal screaming. Trippie has continued to push the boundaries as his career has progressed. He has an incredibly successful discography as a result: all four of his albums debuted in the Billboard Top 5, while his 2019 mixtape *A Love Letter To You 4* topped the chart. "I made my own type of sound," he said. "I just rapped like me. I sang, I rapped, I screamed too. I'm gonna be the best star I can be in whatever genre or wherever they put me."

The people and work that go on to be remembered through time are usually very distinctive. We can't make a true impact by replicating past ideas and events without adding something of our own. Even if we're worried about how others might perceive our ideas, we can always give them a test run in private and build our confidence before sharing them with the world. But we can't allow others to stop us from being distinctive, pioneering, innovative, and, most importantly, ourselves.

CHAPTER FIVE

MENTAL WELLBEING

TAKE TIME OFF

BIG SEAN

As we continue to become successful in what we are doing, it's common to lose sight of why we are doing it from time to time. We can find ourselves doing things because we believe we are supposed to, or because we've become so deeply entrenched in our routine that we no longer ask ourselves why we're doing it. When this happens, it's often an indication that we need to give ourselves some time off, so we can have space to reflect.

After Big Sean put out his fourth solo album *I Decided* and his *Double or Nothing* mixtape with producer Metro Boomin, both in 2017, he intended to stay in the studio and continue the momentum, starting work on his fifth album immediately. However, he soon found that through nonstop productivity, he'd lost sight of his purpose. "Rapping and making music, that's something I always wanted to do, since I was eleven years old," he told me. "And I got to a point where I was feeling very burned out, feeling like it was more of a job than my passion. I had tons of anxiety and just felt inadequate. To the point where I didn't even wanna live anymore."

Big Sean identified a need to reconnect with the feeling he'd had when he first started rapping, before it became a decade-long career, when every Friday night he'd drive to his local radio station to freestyle on air. Sean took some time

away, disrupting his routine, and giving himself the space to wrestle with the questions that often get pushed aside in the middle of a project when deadlines are looming: "I did a lot of spiritual work, connecting with myself, and really analyzed and asked myself, 'What is my passion? Why am I here? What is my real goal?' And I realized that my purpose on Earth is to inspire people." With that in mind, he empowered himself to be more courageous in his subject matter and more candid with his audience than ever before—returning in 2020 with a new catalog staple, *Detroit 2*.

"MY PURPOSE ON EARTH IS TO INSPIRE PEOPLE"

Sometimes we need to find some perspective on what we're doing— whether we've been working for ten minutes, ten days, ten weeks, or a whole decade! To do this we need to be kind to ourselves and allow ourselves to take some time away. While we're doing something else we can trust that our brains are still working in the background, so we can recalibrate and return with purpose, allowing us to take our work to the next level.

TALK TO SOMEONE
BIG SEAN

It's easy for our problems to escalate quickly if we keep them bottled up in our heads. While we can't expect someone else to solve our problems, sharing them—and being listened to—can make a huge difference in helping to put things in perspective. It can shrink our problems and allow us to see them as manageable.

On his 2020 track "Deep Reverence," Big Sean questions why managing anxiety isn't on the school curriculum, despite the fact that it affects so many of us. His own personal struggle with anxiety is something he's been trying to manage before he even understood what it was.

"This is something I deal with on a daily basis," he told me. As an artist who puts a lot of his personal experiences into his work he needed to learn to deal with unsolicited criticism, and as he gained success this issue only became bigger. "My heart is wide open when I'm making my music. So you see criticism, you see hate, you see people judging you and picking you apart, and it's like, I didn't know I gave you permission to even judge me like that."

Over time, Sean has learned to protect himself by remembering that he is in control of his own feelings, which aren't dictated by the perceptions of others. "I realized that the only way somebody can affect how I'm feeling is if I give them permission to make me feel like that," he explained. "I had to just put it all in perspective."

These conclusions and coping mechanisms differ from person to person. They take a lot of work to find, and are generally part of a broader work in progress. To reach this perspective Sean needed to talk his problems through. "I was like, is something wrong with me? On the inside, in my head, and I don't know how to handle it? And I just had to talk to somebody," he recalled.

Sean reached out to a therapist, and began to build a transformative relationship: someone who he could speak with confidentially, who was independent of his personal life. This provided him with the freedom to talk

about and work through various issues without putting too much pressure on those around him. "You can leave it all there [within the boundaries of the therapy session]," he explained. "So that's one of the things that really helped benefit me."

Whether or not we have the means to work with a therapist, it's important when you're struggling with something that you don't keep it to yourself. It's always better to talk about how you're feeling with a trusted friend or family member who is a good listener, rather than to allow things to build up inside. Equally, it is helpful to learn to be a good listener. Just try to take in what is being shared with you and understand what is being communicated, rather than attempting to provide enlightening responses or offer advice in return. More often than not, all we need is for another person to truly understand our point of view and what we're going through.

GET OUT OF YOUR OWN HEAD

NONAME

We can spend a lot of time in our own heads. At times, usually in short bursts, this can lead to creative breakthroughs, problem-solving, and personal growth. However, it's easy to slip from introspection into overthinking if we're not careful. The latter clouds our perspective and often consumes us in a spiral of unhelpful thoughts that can skew our understanding of reality.

Noname gets out of her own head by reading. I spoke with her in 2016, the morning after her first New York headline show, and she admitted she'd been so caught up in her thoughts that she hadn't been able to fully experience her career milestone in the present. "Last night, I wish I could have enjoyed last night a little more. But I was overthinking," she said. "But today I looked back on it and was like, 'Oh shit, that show was kind of raw.'"

Noname said that a method she'd found particularly helpful for getting out of her head was delving into a book. "Reading is dope to get out of your head," she told me. "I'm really into

authors who use a lot of poetic language within normal literature."

"READING IS DOPE TO GET OUT OF YOUR HEAD"

That day, Noname recommended Toni Morrison's novel *Jazz* to fans of her debut mixtape *Telefone*, and reading has become an even bigger focus of Noname's work with the launch of the Noname Book Club in 2019. As a community that exists both on and offline to connect community members inside and outside carceral facilities with radical books, each month the book club highlights books and essays written by Black, Indigenous, and other people of color to their chapters in the United States and the UK. It offers a Prison Program to help make the books available to incarcerated people around the US and suggests Black-owned bookstores and local libraries to help

readers find them. Through the Noname Book Club, Noname is utilizing her passion for reading to have a powerful impact, helping to uplift the voices of those from marginalized backgrounds and building a community that transcends geographical boundaries.

Overthinking is cyclical in nature. We get stuck going round and round over the same thing: trying to justify our worries, running through possible scenarios, and rehearsing our reactions. In times of anxiety or stress, books can allow us some space from our own thoughts. Whatever the purpose of our reading, or our chosen genre, books can really help to disrupt this recurring pattern and bring us back to the reality of a more introspective and helpful approach.

EMBRACE
ESCAPISM
ISAIAH RASHAD

A healthy dose of escapism helps us to reorganize and contextualize our thoughts in a way that's much more manageable than excessive internalizing and overthinking. Identifying with characters and stories that exist outside of our reality allows us to look at our emotions or issues with a degree of separation.

While rap is generally a personal medium, it's also commonly illustrated with surreal, exaggerated references to pop culture, from superheroes to sports stars. During a five-year hiatus between his albums *The Sun's Tirade* and *The House Is Burning*, Isaiah Rashad found refuge in comic books, while working out ways to cope with depression and addiction issues.

In a conversation I had with Isaiah alongside DC Comics writer Tom King and artist Mitch Gerads, the team behind his favorite comic book, *Mister Miracle*, he explained the profound impact their work had made on him: "I probably wouldn't have been able to get through the past couple of years of my life if I hadn't stumbled upon y'all shit," he told them. "It felt like a reflection of my own life. I was so tripped out by how y'all turned this story into some real relatable shit."

Mister Miracle—which Isaiah read while in rehab—deals with main character Scott Free's depression, juxtaposing the high-stakes action of a superhero comic with the mundanity of everyday life, the way we might see it depicted in a melancholic sitcom: "It's hard to make something that serious entertaining," Isaiah praised.

"My experience of depression, putting it on wax and shit, is to put those emotions on there but don't put that word for word experience. My pain isn't entertaining, it's relatable. So I guess that's why I put my shit with music—it's trying to keep that shit entertaining; not fucking listing off why everything sucks."

"MY PAIN ISN'T ENTERTAINING, IT'S RELATABLE"

Although being absorbed by forms of escapism such as books, video games, TV, and movies could mistakenly be deemed unproductive—even by ourselves—it allows us to process our thoughts with a fresh outlook and to see the things we're dealing with in a new way. Whether we're trying to deal with real-life issues, or create engaging and entertaining work, a little reframing can always yield positive results. It's good to allow ourselves the time to escape into something outside of our realities when things are getting a little too heavy.

**MANIFEST
CONFIDENCE**

DREEZY

Developing self-confidence is key to leading a more fulfilling and purposeful life. It is a continuing process that we need to pay attention to, but one that is worthwhile and pays off in a multitude of ways, facilitating stronger relationships and empowering us to achieve our goals.

Music has helped Dreezy develop her confidence. Rapping gave her a voice during high school, where she otherwise kept to herself. "Music made me feel like, 'This is how I stand out,'" she told me. "Everybody got what they're good at, and I was always good at music. I just started working on it more and more, and over time I just knew: y'all can't see me when it comes to rap."

As she's progressed through her career, Dreezy has learned to avoid having backup plans, instead making a commitment to her original intention. "We go for plan A, and we adjust as we go, but we don't abort the mission," she stated. "Stick it through and be confident. A lot of people buy into consistency more than talent. Not everything will go exactly to plan, but it's liberating to accept that this is not necessarily negative. "Everything happens for a reason," said Dreezy. "That gives me super confidence. Don't stress about it, you can't force it, just let life flow."

Dreezy believes that it's important to speak with conviction about our goals. "You will notice when you start speaking

"DON'T STRESS ABOUT IT, YOU CAN'T FORCE IT, JUST LET LIFE FLOW"

stuff into existence; it starts happening," she said. "And then when you expect things to be bad, it's always going to be bad. So just keep your hopes high."

Even when we aren't feeling at our best, speaking with conviction about what we want helps us to be resilient. "I think as a human being, of course we have our moments where you might get discouraged or you might not feel as confident," Dreezy admitted. "But I always snap back into myself and put myself on top of the world."

Finding confidence within ourselves doesn't come to us overnight. It's something that we will always experience in highs and lows. However, by learning to manifest that confidence when we need it and by speaking optimistically about our intentions, we can become more resilient, ready to accept when things don't go our way and perform at our best when they do.

BE KIND TO YOURSELF

YOURSELF

BABY TATE

While the internet makes us aware of how much opportunity is out there, and the greatness that is achievable to us all, this can leave us feeling self-critical and unworthy. It's great to strive towards our goals and have a strong work ethic, but this makes it all the more necessary to also be kind to ourselves and to practise self-love.

Baby Tate told me that her mother always taught her to be kind to herself. Although she believed she was taking the advice on board, in fact she was directing her kindness to others before herself. During the pandemic, while Tate was in lockdown, she began to understand and internalize the meaning of her mother's words. "I see it on social media, people are just dragging themselves: 'I'm so ugly, I'm so fat, I'm so dumb'," she reflected. "The internet is a beautiful place, but it's also a sick and nasty, twisted place full of mean people. If you know that, why would you also do that to yourself? Because people are going to do it anyway."

Tate receives hate from strangers on a daily basis. If she joined them in saying the same negative things to herself, she'd quickly lead herself to a very difficult mental space. Instead, she works to counter these by reinforcing positive beliefs about herself.

"Even if at first it's delusional, you really have to build this border around yourself of love," she said. "And knowing yourself is very important for that. You have to accept yourself so that even if other people don't accept you, it doesn't matter."

We can go through our entire lives without ever truly knowing and accepting ourselves. Even those of us who engage with that work quickly realize that it's a never-ending process. The approach for deepening our knowledge of self will be different for each individual. It's only through experimentation that we can find methods that resonate with us. For Tate, these have included moments of solitude, journaling, affirmations, tarot, and astrology. Others may use meditation, breathing exercises, counselling, life coaching, group therapy, vision boards, physical exercise, or self-help books. Whichever techniques feel good to us will likely reap rewards, but we must be prepared to grind: "It's work," Tate reminded me. "It's not easy. It's a lifelong process, because we change as humans, we're ever evolving."

It's important that we are our own advocates. We must remind ourselves of our strength and power in order to bring balance to what can feel like a constant flow of negativity. Getting to know ourselves as intimately as possible is an ever-evolving process, but ultimately a deeply rewarding one.

CHAPTER SIX
BALANCE

MAINTAIN A GOOD WORK/LIFE BALANCE
BIG K.R.I.T.

Not everything in life needs to be based around work. We can be misled into thinking that productivity has a moral value, but it's vital that we break out of that mode of thinking and allow ourselves to just be. Work is only one part of life, but we often allow it to overpower everything else.

When he turned thirty, Big K.R.I.T. realized that he'd been missing out on so much, due to his obsession with productivity. "Looking back on life, and all my friends have kids, my parents are getting older—my mom's like 'When am I going to have a little grandchild running around here?'" he told me. "And that's real life reminding you, 'Hey, I know you're working and you're goal-oriented, but you still want to live some too, right?'"

The realization that the career success he'd been building toward didn't make him happy motivated K.R.I.T. to enjoy the seemingly simple things in life rather than just rely on the pursuit of career milestones and accolades. "I love hiking, I just like chilling and going outside, and watching the birds. I finally started to experience life myself," he said. "A lot of the things I wasn't really enjoying because I was into my phone or trying to make sure I met a deadline. Now I take the time out to really enjoy my surroundings and express myself to the people that I love."

"I FINALLY STARTED TO EXPERIENCE LIFE MYSELF"

Big K.R.I.T. learned to stop rushing to his phone every time it rang and to detach himself from social media. Instead, he would spend more time with his partner, going for walks around the neighborhood or watching movies. "I'm just taking some time to let things breathe a little," he said. From that balanced perspective he was able to write his independently released double-

album *4eva Is A Mighty Long Time* in 2017, which charted in the Billboard 200 Top Ten. The acclaimed record delves further into the duality of his life as the rapper Big K.R.I.T. and his experiences as civilian Justin Scott.

Even when we feel as though we aren't being productive, our brains are still working for us. Much like an app works in the background on a phone or computer, it doesn't have to be displayed on the screen to be processing something meaningful. Sometimes the best thing we can do is to rest and allow that to happen. Taking time for ourselves is vital for life progression, and it certainly isn't tied to morality, so we never have to explain ourselves or feel guilty when we need rest. If we maintain a good work/life balance, once we come back to our work feeling enriched and revitalized, we'll be ready to make an even stronger contribution than before.

UNPLUGGING IS THE MOVE
SMINO

Our lives are often very noisy. This can be physically, due to the environment we're in or the people we're around, or it could be mentally, because of pressure from work or the endless scrolling of news feeds. Occasionally, this noise can be a necessary part of dealing with a particular issue or completing a task. But if it goes unmonitored and lasts for long periods, this generally leads us to burnout. It's important that we develop self-awareness around how much we engage, so that we know when it's getting too much and find some time to unplug.

Smino tries to find moments of relaxation everyday. "Those little pockets you get in life to where you can actually breathe—it's important to take them and turn them into the most you can," he told me. "And then when you go back to it, you're always refreshed."

"THOSE LITTLE POCKETS YOU GET IN LIFE TO WHERE YOU CAN ACTUALLY BREATHE—IT'S IMPORTANT TO TAKE THEM"

After the overwhelming experience of making his first album, 2017's blkswn, Smino took a mental break, which included taking time away from the Internet and the expectations of those around him. "People always need something from me. Every day, someone is going to ask you for something. Even if it's the slightest thing," he explained. "I was just at the point where I was like, I'm going to cool out, unplug myself from everybody emotionally, and I don't care how anybody feels about this. I'm just going to take this little time."

Taking that time for himself was necessary because of the work demands that he knew were on the horizon, which included rehearsals, video shoots, and touring in support of the record. It gave him the perspective to see how much he was taking on mentally each day, and the understanding that he had to be selective in order to be effective in the things he was engaging with.

"Unplugging is the move," he said. "Even if you're in a relationship with a person, you can be so plugged into the way they feel that it can take a toll on you, and now you're not energized for the shit you need to do. I just learned to just pick and choose when to plug my energy into shit. It took that to realize that I was plugged into so many different sources, and I'm like 'Oh, I've got to just kind of pick and choose, because it's just getting crazy.'"

While it's understandable that we want to support those around us, it's difficult, and at times dangerous, to help others if we're burned out ourselves. There is no reason to feel guilty for taking some time to unplug for a while, whether it's an hour a day or even a longer break after a particularly busy period at work. We must normalize saying no to people when we don't have the capacity to deal with their requests, without the risk of ruining our relationships. Ultimately, we'll be much more present, empathic, and resilient human beings if we can cut through life's noise by successfully managing our own mental capacity.

MAINTAIN A HEALTHY BODY AND MIND

JOE KAY

When we're feeling burned out mentally, a great way to provide some counterbalance is to do some physical activity. This draws us away from the mind and into the body, which helps us clear our head and leaves us feeling rejuvenated. Even after a short amount of exercise or a physical task, we can return to our work with a new perspective.

Soulection cofounder Joe Kay spends his days fielding lots of responsibilities. He's constantly switching hats, from entrepreneur to DJ, community leader to curator. "I try to find that balance of shutting off people, shutting off emails, knowing when to attend the show, or make a presence somewhere," he told me. "The creativity is what keeps me going. The business, the meetings, the emails can really burn me out and give me anxiety."

When Joe started to focus on health and wellness, as a way of coping with his busy lifestyle, it became one of his biggest sources of inspiration outside of music. "I don't think it's talked about enough," he said. "Even if it's 15 to 30 minutes, I'll do push-ups, I'll run, I'll do burpees, just whatever I can. Just to stay healthy, because being on the road and the way you eat, you're drinking, it's not healthy, and it builds a lot of anxiety and stress, so that's been an outlet, working out."

Joe was spending a lot of time on the road, and in the 12 months prior to our conversation had traveled as far as Dubai, South Africa, Russia, India, Australia, and the UK, as well as touring the US. He began to notice bigger artists and DJs having to retire prematurely due to health issues, and took note, motivating the rest of the Soulection crew to get on the same page. "Yo, you guys gotta take care of yourselves," he recalled telling his peers. "If you keep going this way for the next five, ten years, it's going to kill us. It's

"YOU GUYS GOTTA TAKE CARE OF YOURSELVES"

going to take a toll—so that's been another source of inspiration for us [...] staying healthy and fit mentally."

Alongside physical exercise, Joe also ensures that he carves time out of his busy schedule to sit alone with his thoughts. "Giving myself privacy, thinking, writing things down in my notebook—those are the small things that I don't take for granted in life," he said. "I think more people need to do that." He believes that it's vital, no matter how busy we are, to find some time for ourselves and the things that make us happy. "'Are you making time for yourself and for the things that make you happy? And if not, why not?'" he asks. "'If you can make time for something else, if you can make time to build someone else's company or legacy, what are you doing for yourself?' That's the message I try to push."

Life is finite and we can't invest too much of it in the dreams of others. Everything needs to be a part of a bigger picture toward our own self care and self-actualization. Every day, take some time out for yourself, whatever is manageable, even if it's only a few minutes, to do some physical and mental activity that is appropriate to your lifestyle and ability. This will help you to have more balance in your day, autonomy over your life, and contribute to a healthy body and mind.

CHAPTER SEVEN
RELATIONSHIPS

BE EMPATHIC

PHARRELL WILLIAMS

Division has become all too common in our modern world. For tech giants and media conglomerates, polarization is extremely profitable, so we're regularly pitted against those that don't share our ideas or opinions. We are pushed to choose sides, while the nuance and gray areas that would allow us to find commonality and connection are eliminated. The antidote to this separated world is to try to empathize with those who we could see as the opposition—whatever matter it is that we're disagreeing on.

Empathy is the ability to perceive or identify with the way other people are feeling, even if that is not the way we are feeling ourselves. During a conversation we had in London during the summer of 2018, Pharrell Williams told me that he believes empathy is vital to humankind.

"Empathy is the skeleton key to any room," he explained. "It's the number one thing that we need before love. Because if you have no empathy, then you can't even get to why you should love someone else. That goes for the one that you marry, the one that you hate, your parents, your children, strangers. If you have no empathy, it's not possible for you to like and definitely not possible for you to love."

"EMPATHY IS THE SKELETON KEY TO ANY ROOM"

Despite a long and prosperous career that saw him making huge contributions to music, fashion, and culture, Pharrell considers his own "evolution to consider others" to be the achievement he's most proud of. By setting a good example ourselves, he believes that we can introduce others to empathy—to the benefits of working against the division of humanity. "So many institutions and different corporations pander to the things that are divisive—there's a lot of business in things being divisive; there's a lot of money to be made. [But] people can find other ways to make money, besides being divisive. That's what's important for me."

Approaching others with empathy allows us to find commonality with them. This serves as a much better starting point for long-lasting relationships than immediately clashing over the things we don't agree on. We're never going to agree on everything, but we'd all be able to coexist and collaborate much more positively if we tried to identify with the feelings of others, rather than making judgments.

THE TRUE MEANING OF COLLABORATION

NIGO

The word "collaboration" has been overused to the point where it's almost beyond recognition. What once described a truly integral part of humanity is now a buzzword for selling two brands at once. As creative people and human beings, we must reclaim this word from the corporations and reinvigorate it with its true relational power.

Visionary designer, DJ, and pop-culture archivist NIGO reminded me that collaboration is about so much more than marketeers would have us believe. After 20 years away from recording music, he'd been collaborating with some of his friends in the US hip-hop scene—including Pharrell, Kid Cudi, A$AP Rocky, and more—on a new album called *I Know NIGO!*, when I emailed him a question, enquiring what the word meant to him.

"There is a lot of use of that word in the fashion business these days to describe what is really just co-branding," he responded. "I don't find that attractive. If collaboration is to make sense it should be between people working in different areas of specialization. For me, the real meaning of collaboration is to help one another create something that you couldn't otherwise make alone."

> ## "HELP ONE ANOTHER CREATE SOMETHING THAT YOU COULDN'T OTHERWISE MAKE ALONE"

Collaboration is wasted if each party isn't contributing something of real creative value to the partnership. The true meaning of collaboration is asking for help from those around us when we need it, the ones who have skills that we don't, while helping others who are lacking skills that we have. It is about uniting to achieve a common goal that otherwise wouldn't have been possible.

The exchange of information is particularly important in NIGO's practice,

and allows him to work innovatively and broadly across everything, from clothing and music to dining experiences, like his Curry Up restaurant in Tokyo. "For me it's about learning a lot and then mixing what I've learned together to have fun in the process of making things," he shared. "Whatever has absorbed and entertained the creator of a work will emerge in their output. I'm always trying to make something that I've never seen before."

There is much value in learning from our peers. Everyone who we come into contact with has experienced life in a unique way. There is great wisdom to be gained from these differences, whether that be an exchange of skills or sharing stories and ideas which can help us to broaden our perspective. Collaboration, in its true sense, can be an everyday occurrence and is key to living harmoniously with the world around us.

MAKE PEOPLE FEEL COMFORTABLE
COMBAT JACK

It's virtually impossible to get anywhere in life without collaboration. For great collaboration to happen we need to help people to be the best version of themselves. We want people to feel uplifted and inspired when they're around us, and that requires us to provide the optimal conditions—if we want them to let their guard down and be their true selves with us, then we need to do the same in return. Therefore, we need to make people feel comfortable in our presence.

Pioneering podcaster Reggie Ossé, professionally known as Combat Jack, wanted to highlight the success and excellence of his guests, and he knew that comfort was key to bringing out the best in them.

Reggie, who lost his life to cancer in 2017, was a vital player in documenting the culture to which he'd made such a huge contribution. When I spoke to him during a trip to London in the summer of 2016, he admitted that he was still somewhat naive regarding the impact of his work with *The Combat Jack Show*. "I'm a fan," he said, humbly. "When I approach my guests, I'm not trying to tear them down. I want to be inspired, and I want my listeners to be inspired as to what made you great."

In order to provide a situation in which a guest would want to share their most inspirational stories, Reggie knew he had to promote a culture of trust. "I want them to feel comfortable," he explained. "I'm trying to reduce the defensiveness that some of my guests might have and really pull them into this world of enthusiasm that I'm bringing to the table."

In creating a nonjudgmental environment based around empathic listening, genuine enthusiasm, and respect for his guests, *The Combat Jack Show* provided a longform insight into hip-hop culture that was able to cut through the drama and clickbait of the era. Reggie was able to help his guests tell unforgettable stories, pushing the positive narratives that he took from them to the forefront, adding new perspectives, and, in some cases, changing perceptions altogether.

"Recently, I had reality-show phenomenon, Instagram stripper phenomenon, Cardi B on my show," he enthused. "The general, initial reaction, particularly from my core audience that respects my brand is like, 'Yo Combat, what are you doing? Are you falling off? We don't need to hear her perspective.'"

However, Reggie was able to see through the preconceived biases and judgments, and offer an early insight into one of hip-hop's biggest stars. "I wanted her to capture that, so not only could I give her audience what they wanted to hear, but I could give a different perspective to *my* audience. *The Combat Jack Show* audience trust me and after this show respect in terms of how brilliant she is. How much of a survivor, a fighter, a dreamer, and a creator she is."

To create the conditions for great relationships to grow, we must be accepting, genuine, and empathic toward those who we're communicating with. We can try to put these conditions into practice in any conversation or interaction we find ourselves in. Connecting with others in a meaningful way can only come out of an authentic desire to form positive relationships, and these are the ones that will truly make an impact on our lives for years to come.

BE THE ULTIMATE CONNECTOR

GUCCI MANE

When we've worked hard for the successes in our lives, it can be tempting to want to keep them for ourselves. To remind people of our greatness. It might seem counter-productive to use our moment to platform somebody else. But we must consider how we use our power, and not allow our own paranoia and insecurity to prevent us from making a real impact and helping others.

Gucci Mane has never been afraid to share the spotlight. "I always crew up," he told me, during a conversation we had on a Dublin golf course one afternoon in the summer of 2017. "I always get artists and help them."

As a globally respected artist and entrepreneur with a diehard following, Gucci Mane has increased the mark he's made on music and culture through the countless game-changing artists that he has championed. "[There are] so many people that I done helped, from Metro Boomin to the Migos, Nicki Minaj, Young Thug, all these great artists. It's like I've always been a magnet for talent. I feel like that's my strong point," he told me. "That's what I want to be known for like, 'Gucci, he helped so many different people.'"

If we're secure in our own work, then making ourselves an intrinsic part of an active and successful network of people can be very fulfilling. Great careers have been built from being what the author Malcolm Gladwell refers to in his bestselling book, *The Tipping Point,* as a "connector." He defines those with this quality as "people with a special gift for bringing the world together." Gucci, a big fan of Gladwell's work, described himself as "the ultimate connector."

Gucci sees his ability to platform others and bring people together as his legacy. It's allowed him to transcend generations of stars, as he remains a vital cultural touchstone. "I never aspired to be the best artist," he said. "What I value more is longevity. Just don't be a flash in the pan. I'm more proud of being relevant 12 years after I started. To just have people still booking you, still want to collaborate with you, still want to interview you, still want you to be a part of their brand or endorse their product. A lot of people that [were] way bigger than me when I first got in the game, who I looked up to, they gone. After all the years, that's my greatest accomplishment."

Although it's important not to put the needs of others ahead of our own, there are many ways to share our successes and opportunities which allow us to make a positive impact. We can platform work or people that inspire us, recommend people for opportunities that we hear about, and introduce like-minded people to one another. These actions will only help us to expand our own reach and feel connected, as we do our part in bringing the world closer together.

FAMILY IS
EVERYTHING
BOLDY JAMES

Our families play a huge part in shaping who we are. Family can mean different things to each of us, and it's up to us to form our own personal definition. We are relational beings and those we spend our time with, particularly during our formative years, have a lasting effect on the way we see the world. And likewise, although we are often unaware of doing this, we will naturally influence and inspire things in others. While these relationships can become intense, strained, and at times even dysfunctional, spending time with family can be a great way to connect with who we really are.

Though his strong work ethic and prolific release schedule have been key to his career success, Boldy James puts his family first. There have been times when Boldy has pushed rap to the side in order to get his foundations in order. "Family is more important to me than my dreams or my rap career," he told me in 2018, while cruising around Detroit in the bitter cold of winter. "Now that I feel like I've got more structure in my household, I got back to the music."

"FAMILY IS MORE IMPORTANT TO ME THAN MY DREAMS"

No matter how busy Boldy was with late-night studio sessions and touring obligations, every morning was dedicated to getting his kids up, out of bed, and ready for school—even when he was only running on an hour's sleep.

"They're not all morning people, so I go through mixed emotions with each child," he said. "That morning time to take the kids to school, or while I'm at the crib cooking dinner, or I'm on they tail about doing they chores—that's when I feel the most authentic, because that's the real me, the person I am to my children. I can't fake that. You can't lie to your kids. And you got to be the message that you bring, and practice what you preach."

From the pressures of work to the nonstop stream of content that we're being fed by our phones, there are so many things distracting us from the significance of spending quality time with our people. We're often moving so quickly from one thing to another that we forget to take the time to appreciate what family means to us. Unfortunately, it can often take times of difficulty and crisis to bring us together, but we can do our best not to let it get to that. If we are ever feeling out of sorts, or even just in need of some sustenance or inspiration, it can be worth considering spending some time with those closest to us, reconnecting with that feeling of who we are and what we represent within that family unit.

LET PEOPLE KNOW HOW YOU FEEL

SLOWTHAI

At times, often without realizing it, we can set unreasonable expectations for those around us. We want them to be virtually telepathic. Perhaps we're overwhelmed with work and a friend is complaining that we don't make time for them, or maybe we've been struggling with difficult issues at home and our coworkers keep making extra demands on our time. These situations often leave us harboring resentment, despite the fact that no harm was intended. After all, they had no idea how we were feeling. In order to ensure that our relationships remain healthy, we need to learn to communicate our emotions to those around us.

That has been a vital part of slowthai's creative process. As someone who makes vulnerable, emotional music, he's had to learn to be comfortable sharing his feelings with those present in the studio when he's recording—before it can ever reach the ears of his listeners. Sat in the basement studio of his family home one afternoon, he told me that his generally smiley disposition can sometimes mask how he's feeling. "Even when I'm sad, I'm smiling," he divulged. "So I think it's important just letting my friends know, 'Yo man, I'm not actually feeling alright.'" This often leads to a conversation about the root cause of his emotion that day, and allows him to record candidly. "It's just a way I can have confidence in voicing it without feeling like there's little bits I can't say."

It is also important to remember to express our sentiments of love and reverence for our friends, family, and peers. These can go unsaid all too often, and at times lead to feelings of under-appreciation. "I feel like sometimes I neglect people and I don't let them know how much I actually do care for them," admitted slowthai. "So at any chance now I get, I try to let 'em know. You never know, someone's day might be the shittest day ever and that two-second phonemail might make their day a little bit better."

slowthai has felt a natural urge to express his emotions since he was young. However, he admits that at times he felt inhibited by the hyper-masculine expectations of growing up on a British council estate. "I always tried [expressing how I felt about others], but whether I could do it with the people I was around at those moments in time [was another issue]," he explained. "Because of fear of that toxic masculinity. That was always a thing that played part in my life heavily, even though I just thought, 'This shit's stupid.'"

It took some time before slowthai was able to let go of his attachment to how his declarations of admiration would be received by others. "If they don't accept it, I'd still be like, 'Yo, I love you'. If I got love, I got time, I got energy, you mean something to me," he said. "I feel it's important [to voice that] because you never know when your last moments are gonna be."

Sadly, these expressions do not always come naturally in our fast-moving society. However, if we want to improve our relationships, then learning how to communicate our emotions is imperative. If we are able to name our feelings, and have the strength to share them, then we're much more likely to receive the support and understanding that we need from the people in our lives. Furthermore, if more of us develop these skills, then society as a whole will be all the better for it.

CHAPTER EIGHT
PATIENCE

LEARN TO SIT WITH IT
DANNY BROWN

In our increasingly fast-moving world, it's almost become our default setting to put ourselves under pressure. We often feel anxious that there's some kind of deadline looming over everything we do, from watching the latest hit TV series to listening to the latest album releases. We can even find ourselves posting thoughts online before they've even fully formulated in our heads. Everything is becoming a shared experience that we need to take part in right now, or feel like we've missed out.

It is generally more rewarding not to engage in this kind of behavior. Taking things in our own time and on our terms allows for a more enriching experience. Having time to allow our thoughts to fully form, and to consider opposing points of view before we share them with the world, is essential.

Danny Brown hasn't allowed himself to get caught up in the rush. "In my world, when I was a kid I remember my favorite artists would take two, three years [to release an album] maybe," he told me. "I just don't even get caught up in that world."

At that point Danny was preparing to release *Atrocity Exhibition*, a record he'd taken three years to make while most of his peers were releasing albums at least annually—with many churning out mixtapes and EPs on top. Danny talked about the need to sit with his music, so that he could understand its ability to evolve as time passed.

"I might make [a song] and I might not really like it like that," he said. "Then, three months later, it's fucking amazing. But [if] I would have been trying to release an album and making them in one month, that probably would have been a song to scratch and never [release]."

Danny watched the way that the hard-labored work of his peers was being consumed, often worked on for 12 months just to receive a fortnight's worth of recognition, and he didn't want to get caught up in the same cycle. "I want my albums to mature, more than just the talk of two weeks. That's what you see on the Internet now: It's the best album in the world for two weeks and then ain't nobody talk about it. With me, I'd rather skip all the hype and then tell me a year later. Sit with it, let it mature..."

Danny's patience with his work gives his music a certain timelessness. It doesn't conform to the sonic trends of the period and it holds up to repeated listens, revealing new ideas and meaning for the listener even years beyond its release. "I take a lot of pride in making sure that [my music] maintains its value," said Danny. "A lot of music depreciates itself in time. Just by being trendy. I just want to make something that I know ten years later, 20 years later, you could still tell that this was something special."

If we want to live in an intentional way, we can't pace ourselves according to the tempo of those around us. If a TV show is worth watching, it will still be worth watching when we get around to it on our own time. Similarly, for something we're making to have value, we should take the time we need to work on it, without feeling pressured by a societal deadline to rush it out. Our thoughts must be given time to develop, before being instantly shared. Sitting with things helps us to take stock of our feelings and the context in which we're living, thinking, and creating. Giving things the time they need and deserve will lead to a more purposeful existence.

LET THEM CATCH UP

FUTURE

If we are committed to originality, the work we're making or the way we're presenting ourselves can be ahead of their time. This means we can be misunderstood or underappreciated by others, which is difficult to swallow.

> ## "FROM THE BEGINNING UNTIL NOW, I JUST CONTINUED TO WORK AND PEOPLE GOT USED TO IT"

However, it's important that we remain confident in our stance, true to ourselves, and remember that people will come around eventually.

When I interviewed Future in 2014, ahead of the release of his second album *Honest*, he was already developing ideas for *FUTURE* and *HNDRXX*—which would eventually be released as a pair of albums a week apart three years later.

"When I was recording I didn't want it to sound like anything that was out at the time," he described of the music he'd been making. "I wanted to go for more of an adventurous and eclectic sound."

Two months into working on the albums, he decided to put them on ice. "*FUTURE* and *HNDRXX* were ahead of their time," he explained. "I wanted to wait, because the records that I was doing felt like the people wouldn't get it as much."

So Future went back to the drawing board to make *Honest*, which would bridge the gap until he eventually had everything aligned to fully realize *FUTURE* and *HNDRXX* as two different sides of his sound—which became a career-defining moment when both albums reached number one in two consecutive weeks.

A pioneer for the contemporary sound of trap, which has had a huge influence on mainstream music and crossed over into pop, R&B, and alternative music, Future was never afraid to be different. His work wasn't

always received in the way that he wanted it to be, but by staying true to himself and his music, he was able to stand strong and wait for others to catch up. "Everything that I do is intentional," he told me. "It's been the driving force of my whole career. Everything that I did, I just work hard for it and work at it, stay consistent."

While he was establishing himself, Future's approach had been to keep a high volume of material in circulation:

"One year, I dropped like 12 mixtapes and had over 20 songs on the radio," he said. "From the beginning until now, I just continued to work and people got used to it... you have to roll it out and wait for it."

The need for external approval or validation can inhibit our progress. But if we have faith in our judgment, we can liberate ourselves from these limitations. By trusting ourselves and allowing others to catch up later, we can be creative, innovative, even visionary.

LEARN FROM THE JOURNEY
SNOH AALEGRA

If we spend too long focusing on our ambitions, we can make the mistake of overlooking what is happening right in front of us. We can miss out on valuable experiences or underappreciate small achievements. Everything happens for a reason and can have value if we take the time to soak it in. It's important to remember that everything is a process, and even if things aren't going in the direction we'd prefer, we can always learn from the journey.

Snoh Aalegra enjoyed a huge career breakthrough in 2019 with her second album *Ugh, those feels again*. When she released the album she was 31, but she'd been making music since she was nine years old.

"I was into music at that very early age and I was very inspired by the music I was hearing," she told me in 2014, around the release of her debut EP, *There Will Be Sunshine*. "My mom was playing a lot of soulful music, a lot of Stevie Wonder, Michael Jackson, Whitney Houston—I remember hearing these artists and it would give me goosebumps listening to them, and I was like 'Wow! I want to do that. How they make me feel, I want to make other people feel.'"

At the age of 14, she signed a development deal with Sony Music Sweden which lasted for a few years, although she'd eventually leave the label without releasing any music. Several years later, she'd have some national success, releasing a studio album under her middle name, Sheri, in 2010 before moving to Los Angeles. "I've been through the whole cliché journey of being with the right people, being with the wrong people, going through all that mess," she told me. "It really taught me a lot and made me the person I am today, so I'm grateful for that experience."

By the time we spoke in 2014, she was still five years from the success of *Ugh, those feels again*, but already had the patient demeanor that allowed her music to grow steadily to where it is today. "I'm a new artist, nobody knows about me," she said. "So I don't want to shove stuff in people's faces like 'Listen

> ## "IT REALLY TAUGHT ME A LOT AND MADE ME THE PERSON I AM TODAY, SO I'M GRATEFUL FOR THAT EXPERIENCE"

to this!' It's better if you let it grow organically, I want to let it be there, let people share it."

Snoh has learned from each step of her journey, and as a result has built a career centered around music that is authentic to her. "You'll get a piece of me listening to the music, more than you would get maybe meeting me the first time, because I'm kind of [an] introvert," she told me. "If you want to get to know me a little bit quicker than face to face, listen to my music!"

Whatever is happening in our lives it's helpful to work on staying as present as possible. Every step of our journey through life is an opportunity to learn something about ourselves, and even the smallest achievements need to be acknowledged in some way. Each of these experiences will cumulatively make a contribution toward honing our approach and helping us find the route that works best for us.

THE POWER OF BOREDOM

BABY TATE

Boredom often feels like something to be avoided. Many of us fill our time as much as possible, terrified of being left alone with nothing to do. But what if we saw boredom as something to be embraced, rather than feared? Space and time allow us to notice the things that pass us by when we're too busy. It also gives us the opportunity to follow our whims and be creative, and it can potentially lead us to life-changing discoveries.

Baby Tate might never have become an artist without the power of boredom. Growing up as an only child in a single-parent household, she spent a lot of time having to entertain herself. One summer, when Tate was 13, rather than going to camp or staying with her grandparents, she remained at home and spent the majority of her time alone while her mother was working.

With nothing to do, Tate began experimenting on GarageBand. She'd had an interest in music for some time, and had been taking piano lessons, but suddenly looking at the music production software all of her ideas started to make sense. "That is where I was really able to first allow my creativity to just flow," she told me. "Everything that was ever in my head as far as jingles and melodies and harmonies, to explore those things."

Tate began producing beats and recording her own raps and songs, and made seven unreleased albums during her teenage years. A fiercely independent emerging act, she wrote, produced, and engineered her first three records, establishing herself as an all-round musical talent before going on to collaborate with other producers and writers.

Tate laments the fact that boredom has become such a rarity in today's society. "We don't allow ourselves to be bored, especially now," she said. "There's always some stimulation, whether you're on your phone, you're watching TV, or listening to some music. Some people are actually afraid of silence, and because I was able to have that, I was able to silence my own mind, and quiet myself, to

hear these melodies, to hear 'I want to make this music.'"

Tate believes boredom is a necessity for leading creative and fulfilling lives. "To be idle, they say, is the devil's playground, but I think that it's really creativity's playground. Because if you're not idle, if you're always doing something, you can't really just sit back and think about what you want to do," she explained. "My boredom caused me to want to make music for the rest of my life, and if it wasn't for me having nothing to do that summer, I don't know if I'd be here right now."

> ## "MY BOREDOM CAUSED ME TO WANT TO MAKE MUSIC FOR THE REST OF MY LIFE"

It's helpful to resist filling every waking moment and to allow ourselves the space to find boredom. Rather than fearing time that isn't already dedicated to an activity, or doing whatever we can to avoid spending time alone, regard these periods as opportunities to be playful and creative. In these moments we can follow our whims and curiosities and listen to our thoughts, without being clouded by the demands of being busy.

CHAPTER NINE

FOCUS

FOCUS ON WHAT'S IMPORTANT
NAS

With so much to engage with everywhere we look, we can easily become distracted from our goals and ambitions. There are so many different ways to measure and perceive success that we can sometimes find we've fallen down a rabbit hole and are in pursuit of something that wasn't important to us in the first place. These are usually forms of external validation, such as aspiring toward the lifestyle of a successful artist, rather than fulfilling our inner need to make great art. With so much going on that's outside our control, we really need to know ourselves and have a strong sense of self in order to be able to prioritize the things that really matter to us, and make our difference there.

When Nas' first album, *Illmatic*, came out in 1994, it wasn't the smooth release that Columbia Records were hoping for from the prodigious Queens rapper they'd signed. "The bootlegging was crazy," Nas recalled, when I talked to him around its 20th anniversary in 2014. "It was everywhere, months before it was even released. There were bootlegs everywhere, not even with the cover or anything. Just tapes, just copies of the album." MC Serch, who was an executive producer on the album, claimed to have found 60,000 copies in a garage prior to the album's release.

Many would be devastated by this. It would undoubtedly damage the sales figures and the clout that came with those numbers. But Nas wasn't focused on that—he was just happy he'd made art that was resonating with others. "When it comes to making your music, you make your music and whenever it comes out, you can't worry about that," he said. "I can drop it, it can leak before, it doesn't matter as long as I'm really proud of what I've put out."

Illmatic is now considered one of the greatest rap albums ever made, and has inspired expanded rereleases, tours, documentaries, and books decades after its release. As hip-hop's reach has continued to expand, listening to the record has become a rite of passage for many, as new generations discover its genius. The work that Nas just wanted to

be proud of continues to find new relevance. "It was already out there for almost a year before the actual release, so it's like that all over again to some extent," he said of the album's 20th-anniversary rerelease. "It's a celebration of a place where I can look back at my life and think about how grateful I am."

When things aren't quite going to plan, or we're feeling distracted, we must remind ourselves of the things that truly motivate us and make them a

"I CAN LOOK BACK AT MY LIFE AND THINK ABOUT HOW GRATEFUL I AM"

priority. It's impossible to be in control of every aspect of our lives, so we have to decide on the things that we are able to control, and then keep our focus trained on those.

PAY ATTENTION TO DETAIL
ANDERSON .PAAK

Often the things that help us to progress aren't huge diversions from what we're doing already. Small details can be incredibly impactful; simple flourishes help to elevate and push us to the next level. While it may be tempting to skip a few steps, details are noticed and appreciated, like taking the time to beautifully wrap a gift for a loved one.

Anderson .Paak had a huge career breakthrough once he realized that all he needed to do was start paying attention to the details.

He'd been recording and releasing work under the moniker Breezy Lovejoy while starting a family. He told me in 2015 that he felt as though he was in a transitional time, and began to start taking his writing and vocal approach more seriously.

"I wanted to do something that hadn't been done," he said. "I wanted my sound to be unique to myself and I wanted a voice that nobody else had. I spent a lot of time developing that and when I came up out of it I wanted to drop the moniker Breezy Lovejoy and just go with my real name; my last name and my middle name."

The "." that comes before Paak is a reminder of that attention to detail—it forces a pause to reflect on the fact that he is an artist who puts thought into everything he does. This ethos was strengthened further when he started working with Dr. Dre, contributing to six songs on the legendary producer's *Compton* album, which began a creative partnership that would expose him to a huge new mainstream audience.

"He's a real perfectionist," said Anderson. "I just feel there's a difference between when I'm working with him and when I'm just recording myself. I can hear the difference in my vocal approach." Experiencing Dre's perfectionism first-hand reinforced Anderson's belief that seemingly small touches can become vital improvements. "It's just pushing for the best, the very best you can do: putting 100% into every take," he reflected. "I think most important is the attention to detail: mixing, the way you record, the way you produce, the mixing, the art, everything."

By putting that extra bit of care into his work, Anderson .Paak has been able to command the respect of people from all over the musical community. From underground heroes to pop icons, nobody can dispute his craft and artistry. "I wanted to have no ceilings and no boundaries to who I can collaborate with or what sounds I can dip into," he told me. "As long as it was good music, then I'm down for it. I wanted to be that kind of artist where they could work with all of these different people and it [would] still make sense."

"I WANTED TO HAVE NO CEILINGS"

When looking for ways to level up, we shouldn't overlook the smaller adjustments we can make to the things we're already doing. Sometimes a drastic change may be in order, but usually this isn't the case. Before rushing back to the drawing board, it's worth considering how paying some attention to the details could be the difference between good and great.

DELIVER THE BEST PRODUCT YOU CAN

RICK ROSS

When we're excited about our goals drawing closer, we can become complacent and cut corners. When success feels tangible, we can forget what got us there in the first place. Whatever it is we're doing, we must always ensure that quality is at its core and we should never compromise on the factors that got us to where we are.

Despite being known for living a luxurious lifestyle, documented through his extensive catalog, Rick Ross told me that the quality of the product is always more important than the profit. Always focused on quality, Ross recalled that from a young age he paid more attention to the work that goes into rap music than those around him.

"I always just loved it more than maybe a normal motherfucker," he remembered. "I just kept the CD covers a little more. You know, when you get up and shit on the toilet in the morning, you read your CD covers for the eight hundredth time? I might've [done] that more."

That care and attention continued into his own writing, and he never lost sight of it as his artistic responsibility began to broaden from writing rhymes to designing packaging and shooting videos. "At first it was just about writing a dope verse, then writing a dope hook on a dope beat, then altogether," he explained. "Now it's all that. I'm still stacking shit on top of that, it ain't just the raps. It's us writing the treatments to the videos. Us having our own film crew, our own directors. Hopefully that's what I'm inspiring [in] the youngsters who are watching."

When I spoke with him in 2014, Ross was between the releases of two albums he dropped that year, *Mastermind* and *Hood Billionaire*. Both are very different records, and speak to different aspects of what his fans love about him. He described *Mastermind* as "more lyrical, wordy, soulful sample-ish" and regarded *Hood Billionaire* "the total opposite," explaining that he wanted it "to most definitely lean toward the South." He'd been spending more time in Memphis and was inspired by the music he loved from there. "It's more catchy, rap-a-longish-type rhymes versus being wordy rhymes," he said. Ross said that he didn't consider the content to be comparable; both albums suit their own moods. "It's whatever zone I'm [in] or what I'm feeling," he said, before referencing other distinct records from his discography. "I might be in a *Deeper Than Rap* type of day, but then again I may be in a *God Forgives, I Don't* kind of day."

What these albums share is their quality of execution. They may each have different purposes, but it's clear that equal amounts of care and attention went into their creation. Ross took heed of what fans were looking for, and delivered excellent products. "Really, it's just all about your fans and giving them what they want. Fans love me for different types of vibes and energy," Ross reflected. "More important than the profit, [is] the product! And the only way you're going to get the best product is whatever drew me to you as an artist."

In those moments of complacency we have to consider what it is that makes us engaging and what we represent, and then deliver that to the highest level we can. In the end, we'll be happier with the results and rewarded with the longevity that's reserved for artists who truly care about making and delivering quality work.

WORK SMALL
GUAPDAD 4000

It's exciting to dream big and have huge aspirations for ourselves, but if we constantly think about these mammoth goals, it's bound to become overwhelming. A helpful way to deal with this is to break down our broader vision into smaller, more manageable chunks. This allows us to work on lots of achievable short-term goals which all contribute toward the bigger picture.

Guapdad 4000 has benefited from working small. Since being diagnosed with attention deficit hyperactivity disorder (ADHD) in his late twenties, he's learned that breaking down tasks helps him to stay happy as he progresses toward his ambition.

Having struggled with depression and mood swings throughout his life, Guap says he became aware that he didn't think in the same way as most of his friends. Although he'd share how he felt, he often wasn't taken seriously by others. So he began working on himself in order to understand why he was so prone to psychological distress. During a conversation with a friend, it was suggested that he might have ADHD, so Guap went to a doctor and was diagnosed.

"It's a spectrum," he told me. "I'm one of those dudes that's affected heavily. I can get stuck for days and not be able to execute anything. Things that affect my career, my happiness, my love life, my family. So much has connected from that realization, it's just changed everything in my life."

Prior to being diagnosed, he had encountered difficulties that he now realizes were all linked to ADHD, but at the time had no explanation for. "They have eaten at my relationships, the way I communicate, the way I love," he said. "I live in my own world which is great because I can create. But I get lost in this shit. I have to remind myself to do basic human things all the time. But when I do it and I stay on top of it, it's been the best experience for me. I feel a lot more complete."

While he can spend hours hyperfocused on one task, he sometimes finds it impossible to do something that many people would find minor, such as send a text message or join a work call. This could lead to issues for him, but he's now able to communicate about it—by being honest and transparent about how he's feeling and the issue it's causing.

Guap advised me that whatever it is we're working to achieve in our lives, the key is to "work hilariously small". He explained, "If you wanna cook, just go and get some salt and pepper, start putting that on the food. If you wanna work out, start by just getting on the ground and doing a push-up. Don't start with [trying to make Lil Wayne's] *Tha Carter III*, start with your mixtape phase. If you have a horrible relationship with your mom and you want to build it out, just start by sending her one emoji."

By working small we're able to make progress without being daunted by expectations of ourselves that we couldn't possibly deal with in the here and now. If we break our bigger macro goals into manageable micro tasks we can achieve in the present, even ones that seem hilariously small, we can feel assured that they all contribute to the future we're building for ourselves. What's more, we can find happiness in that progress.

INTEGRITY IS TIMELESS
FREDDIE GIBBS

With so much access to sources of inspiration, and a lower barrier to entry for many creative practices than ever before, we can find ourselves overwhelmed by the seemingly limitless options for creativity. Experimentation is vital, though it's also worth spending some time considering who we are, what we want to say, and what our most effective methods are for delivering that information.

It's important that we are able to take a critical view of our options. We need to be able to differentiate between what we like and what we make. Just because we love the way that someone else does something doesn't necessarily make it appropriate or necessary for us to bring this into our own work. We must be able to make decisions based on what is right for us, and never allow indecision—and the pressure to try and do everything at once—to overtake our ability to establish identity. The work that will truly stand the test of time is achieved through a balance of pushing our limits while retaining our integrity: being the best version of ourselves.

When Freddie Gibbs released his Madlib-produced *Piñata* album, he knew it had huge potential. "I think it can instantly be a classic," he told me. "The content on it is timeless."

In many ways *Piñata* was the most traditional rap album that Freddie had made by this point. "When it comes to street rap, gangsta rap, I think I got it down to a science. Nobody do it how I do it," he said, acknowledging that Madlib's obscure sample-driven beats weren't in line with what the rest of the rappers in his space were working with at the time. "I think I can have my own lane in it."

"NOBODY DO IT HOW I DO IT"

Freddie was confident that by making good music, it didn't matter what else was going on around him. He'd been writing vivid accounts of street life for years at this point, and had found an iconic cult producer who helped him to really push that lyrical content to the forefront. The album was never going mainstream, but he'd doubled down on the intricacy and specificity that made him Freddie Gibbs. He was no longer competing with anyone else around him, and he'd made something that would last.

"I'm rapping about the streets," he stated. "There ain't too many guys that can cover that front to back like I can. It's a lot of street n****s, but they're not as talented poets as I am, and there's a lot of fucking poets and they're definitely not as street as I am. I bring that shit together the right way."

The approach paid off, and not only was *Piñata* critically acclaimed, but Freddie would also continue to deepen his work with sample-based beats, following up with Madlib on *Bandana* and later receiving a Grammy nomination for his Alchemist-produced *Alfredo* album.

We must have the confidence to stay true to our gut feelings and do what is right for us. We can't allow ourselves to be pulled away by a gimmick that will only last a few months. It's much more satisfying in the long run to create things that resonate deeply within ourselves: even if they don't fit with what our peers are working on. Integrity will always stand the test of time.

CHAPTER TEN
RESILIENCE

HARD WORK BEATS TALENT, WHEN TALENT DOESN'T WORK HARD
KEHLANI

Talent is a gift, but rarely will it allow us to cruise to success with ease. It's important to acknowledge that we will be required to put in the necessary work in order to achieve our goals. Nothing that is truly worth having comes to us without difficulty. Overcoming adversity is what makes us great, and if we want to achieve our goals, then we needn't be discouraged by this: we can find it within ourselves to embrace the challenge and face it head on.

Kehlani is an incredibly talented singer, songwriter, and dancer, but it's unlikely they'd have become a globally renowned, Grammy-nominated act without putting in the years of hard work that it took to break through.

When I spoke with Kehlani in January 2016, they were 20 years old and yet to release an album, but already had the star mentality that's made them the artist they are today. They had laid an impressive amount of ground work for their burgeoning career: appearing on *America's Got Talent* as part of girl group Poplyfe, releasing two acclaimed solo mixtapes, and touring with G-Eazy in the US before selling out two shows in London.

Kehlani had been motivated by the famous saying, "Hard work beats talent, when talent doesn't work hard." The phrase was coined by a high school basketball coach called Tim Notke, and has since been popularized by NBA superstar Kevin Durant.

Early in their career Kehlani identified that there are thousands of others who share similar talents all over the world. They could not expect to succeed on talent alone: to reach their potential would take a combination of talent and work ethic. That doesn't mean pushing ourselves to the point of exhaustion, but looking after ourselves and having the self-awareness to make choices that will benefit our goals. "I have a lot of self-discipline. I know when I'm getting sick and losing my voice and I need to go to sleep," Kehlani said. "We wanted to perform at our best every night, so we're making sure that we were healthy and staying positive, staying able the whole time. This is an industry where opportunities are never handed to you. Doors will be opened, but if you don't step up and meet that, they'll close real fast."

Kehlani made sure that they were always ready, and remained open to facing challenges and overcoming obstacles. "There's going to be lots of no's, lots of closed doors, and people telling you that you can't do it," they explained. "There's going to be so many times that you want to give up. But anything is possible and you never know what could happen tomorrow."

> **"ANYTHING IS POSSIBLE AND YOU NEVER KNOW WHAT COULD HAPPEN TOMORROW"**

It's important to be sure we aren't relying on talent alone to get us by, and that we are prepared to do the work that will allow us to get the most out of our abilities. This means looking after ourselves first and foremost, so that when an opportunity presents itself we're primed and ready to make the most of it.

DON'T BE DISCOURAGED
ACTION BRONSON

There are many factors that can discourage us from pursuing our dreams, many of which are based on perception. Often the most powerful detractors come from within; self-doubt creeps up on us, and we talk ourselves out of doing anything that involves risk, playing it safe and remaining where we are. Sometimes this can also come from others who convince us that our aspirations are too far-fetched, which is usually fueled by their own insecurities. If we allow ourselves to internalize this discouragement, we can become stagnant and limit our opportunities.

Action Bronson has consistently proven those perceptions wrong. A modern-day renaissance man, he started out as a chef, and as the legend goes, started taking rap seriously when he had a broken leg and wasn't able to work in the kitchen. After breaking through on the New York rap scene, he became a global touring act, filming the food show, *Fuck, That's Delicious*, on his travels. He's since taken up painting, written *New York Times* bestsellers, and documented his fitness journey as he overcomes struggles with health, food addiction, and self-acceptance.

Bronson refuses to be put in a box. Despite having redefined himself time and again, each new venture brings its doubters; those who discovered Bronson at some point in his career and would rather he stays there. "I feel like if you do one thing, they always want you to do one thing," he explained. "But they don't know what you have until you show it. So if someone thinks they have you pegged and they don't want to allow you to grow and do what you want, get away from them and don't be involved. You [need] to have in your own mind, and know in your own heart, what you want. Just go for shit. Don't be discouraged."

It isn't always easy. He recalled having the opportunity to appear in the Oscar-nominated Martin Scorsese movie, *The Irishman*, alongside Robert De Niro, admitting that he was "scared shitless." He was likely experiencing imposter syndrome, but he went for it anyway. "If you want to live this life and you have

dreams and aspirations, you gotta go for
it," he said. "What I learned about myself
is that I'm meant to be anywhere I am. It's
not a mistake why I'm there and it's not a
mistake why people ask me to be there."
Bronson continually proves he is capable
of things that his day-one fans would
never have expected. "I think I'm a prime
example of how not to be discouraged by
things," he said. "You wouldn't peg me to
be the typical [guy who's] going to make it
from the New York rap scene. Or an actor

or a fucking fitness guru. I'm a prime
example that things can happen if you
just try. You have to show up."

When we're faced with doubt—
whether it be imposter syndrome or the
perception of others—we must find it
within ourselves to push through, and do it
anyway. This starts with showing up.
There's no reason we won't be able to
succeed in whatever new pursuit we've
become interested in, but it'll never
happen if we don't try.

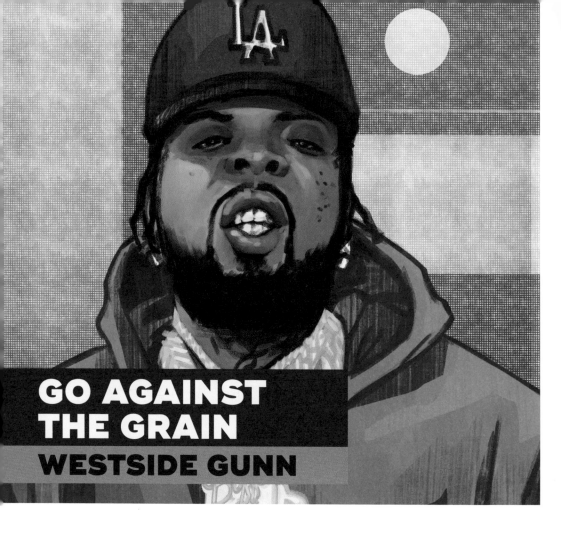

GO AGAINST THE GRAIN
WESTSIDE GUNN

If we pursue what we believe is popular or profitable, rather than what we're passionate about, we are already fighting a losing battle. By conforming, we become part of the status quo, another one of many doing their best to stand out among countless others who are all vying for the same attention. But if we remain a big fish in a smaller pond, we can lead a much more fulfilled and sustainable life.

When Westside Gunn started releasing mixtapes prolifically in the early 2010s, his intricate, grimy, boom-bap sound felt as though it was a universe away from the mainstream music of the time. A decade later, around the release of his acclaimed 2020 album *Pray for*

Paris, he recalled watching the hard-working lyricists around him painstakingly crafting their verses, with little reward, while others would show up in the studio partying and making throwaway records that would end up in regular rotation on the radio, often becoming global hits.

"I have friends on both sides," he told me. "And it's just not fair." While he isn't judgmental about the latter and is personally a big fan of trap music, he made it his mission to shine a light on those keeping the legacy of those detail-focused writers alive. "I have to put some awareness on this style of music, on these types of artists. That's my job in this industry, to make that balance."

Westside Gunn doubled down on making consistent, high-quality records that indulge in East Coast traditionalism, both as a solo artist and through Griselda Records, a label that he founded independently to platform artists around him, such as his brother Conway the Machine and cousin Benny the Butcher. His specific brand of rap incorporated references to his other interests, including high fashion and professional wrestling, into his street narratives, attracting the attention of more people who joined his ever-growing fanbase.

By the time I talked to him from his Atlanta home in 2020, he was able to declare, without exaggeration, that "the raw boom-bap, it hasn't been this respected in two decades. It's happening now. It had to take Griselda to come back to make this happen." The slow build of his connoisseur-focused approach infiltrated the mainstream: without having to compromise their sound, Griselda had released an album through Eminem's Shady Records and signed a management deal with Jay-Z's Roc Nation. Drake was talking about them in interviews, LeBron James was playing their music before games, Virgil Abloh invited them to Paris Fashion week where they soundtracked a runway show, and Kanye West invited them to Wyoming to talk about clothing designs. Westside Gunn never went mainstream—the mainstream came to him.

"That was my goal from day one," said Westside Gunn. "But now people actually see that it worked. It's like, 'Wait a minute, I can actually rap over Alchemist and DJ Premier and still sit front row at the fashion show. I can still have Jay-Z come to my concert?' This is opening up people's eyes, this is the balance."

Trends change, things go in and out of style, so if we're always chasing, the status quo will have moved on by the time we catch up. No matter how far away from the mainstream we feel, we shouldn't fear going against the grain.

BE OPEN TO
OPPORTUNITY

WIZ KHALIFA

Our minds are constantly wandering. Sometimes we're taking a trip down memory lane, transfixed by things that have already happened; other times we're future-tripping, trying to envisage and rehearse scenarios that we may be faced with in times to come. But by trying to recreate events from our past or to manufacture those that haven't yet happened, we can travel through life blinkered from the opportunities that actually do present themselves to us.

Wiz Khalifa has followed an unorthodox career path by staying open to change and the opportunities it brings. "Knowing my position in the game as a leader, as a trendsetter, I can't ever limit myself to anything," he told me during in 2014. "I always have to be ready to expand and broaden."

"AS A TRENDSETTER, I CAN'T EVER LIMIT MYSELF TO ANYTHING"

Wiz was one of the pioneers of online fanbase building when he started making his music freely available, which allowed him to tour and build the global Taylor Gang movement that helped him propel his music into the mainstream. He's continually pivoted into new spaces, building a multifaceted career that includes bonafide hit singles, cult classic mixtapes, movie roles, a co-headline tour with Fall Out Boy, and entrepreneurial ventures, including his own "Khalifa Kush" strain of medical marijuana.

Wiz's Taylor Gang Entertainment record label helped to launch the career of Ty Dolla $ign and bring a new generation of fans to rap legend Juicy J. Outside of his work, he is a father and disciplined practitioner of Muay Thai.

Wiz lives such a full life by trusting the path he's on. "That's one of the most important things to me," he said. "To keep reinventing and stay focused on what's in front of me and not what's behind me."

While it's important to evaluate successes and failures, and to set goals, replaying or imagining events like a video reel becomes unhelpful. We can't alter what's happened before, nor can we predict what's to come. We need to trust that we are exactly where we are supposed to be at this moment, doing precisely what we're supposed to be doing. Engaging in the here and now is the best way to allow ourselves to grow and evolve. All that we truly have control over in any one moment is what we have in front of us, so to be at our most fruitful we must stay present and remain open to surprise.

CHAPTER ELEVEN
CURIOSITY

BE A STUDENT OF THE GAME
NIPSEY HUSSLE

New and inspiring things to learn can come to us in a multitude of ways: Books, documentaries, podcasts, school, even our own conversations. Whether or not we're enrolled in any kind of formal education, we can remain lifelong students, following our curiosities and interests and then reflecting on how our new findings can impact our own lives.

Nipsey Hussle was a true student of the world around him. He was revered and respected among his peers, who have carried on his legacy since he was tragically killed in 2019. Nipsey made an irreversible impact on his community and the world in his short time. I had the honor of talking to him in February 2018, the week he released his Grammy-nominated debut album *Victory Lap*, while he was running errands around LA.

Reading was always an important part of Nipsey's process: he cited Jonah Berger's bestselling 2013 book, *Contagious: Why Things Catch On,* as the inspiration behind his game-changing #ProudToPay scheme, which saw him selling a thousand copies of his Crenshaw mixtape for $100 each. Jay-Z particularly respected the concept, reaching out to Nipsey and buying 100 copies himself.

"My mom raised me in a house full of books," Nipsey remembered. "No matter what my mom was going through financially, if I said, 'I want to get a book,' she'd take me to the bookstore." That thirst for knowledge extended to the online space: "I went to the University of Google," he proclaimed.

Nipsey identified intersections between the subjects that he read about. He realized he could look beyond the immediate world that he inhabited for the answers he needed to succeed in his musical and entrepreneurial endeavors. "We're students of the game. You don't just study music to understand music," he explained. "You start to see the little nuances and the little fibers that connect everything, and I just became really inspired by just seeking out truth."

From reading David R. Hawkins' *Power vs. Force*, Nipsey developed his communication skills to be more focused around this search. "When I deal with people and we're having a disagreement, I question myself like, 'Are you arguing this to be right? Or are you really trying to reveal the truth here?'"

Nipsey also talked about the importance of conversation, and how talking to his peers contributed to the making of *Victory Lap*: a discussion with Hit-Boy about which equipment to invest in, a chat with Lyor Cohen about what separates success and failure in the music industry, and a dialogue with Puff Daddy about how the Notorious B.I.G. managed to communicate his authentic self to pop stardom.

"I'm privileged to be able to have those type of people in my circle, and for [us] to be able to sharpen each other and have a convo," he said. "I've got two ears and one mouth, so we gotta listen twice as much as we talk. And I'm around people that have succeeded in the space that I want to succeed [in], so I listen, I ask questions."

We can approach life with a student mentality and be open-minded in our quest for knowledge. Rather than sticking within our own bubbles we can have a much richer understanding of life by drawing from sources from outside our own direct specialism—listen, ask questions and read broadly—to see how they can enhance our own thinking.

EMBRACE CHANGE
PUSHA T

Ideas move fast. There's always a new style, sound, or software update to keep up with. We need to be able to embrace change without chasing trends and understand how each new development impacts what it is that we do, without allowing it to compromise our core. This requires us to be passionate about the wider context in which we work and not only obsessed with what we do. It's about standing strong in our power, without condemning those who are moving differently.

Nobody knows that better than Pusha T, who's built a career by staying true to himself while embracing the newness that hip-hop offers on a seemingly hourly basis."It's an everyday search for new artists and producers," he told me in 2016, of his role as the President of G.O.O.D Music, the label founded by Kanye West in 2004. "That's part of what I love about hip-hop: the constant creating, the constant search, the embracing of new ideas and ways to expand the genre."

Pusha has retained his relevance for over two decades by valuing, and surrounding himself with, the innovation that comes with each new generation of creators. "It's just different. I feel like the quality is still the same," he explained. "I've been out, I've lived through all of these waves, and really lived in the world. Not only did I buy the music, I rode around to the music. I went to the club, I went to the shows. I've witnessed all of these changes and it's just a different time."

Pusha's open-mindedness has led him to collaborate broadly with artists that transcend generation and genre. But when it comes to his own creative practice Pusha doesn't compromise. "People will see the difference between what it is that I do and what everyone else does," he said. "I don't think anyone is really rapping at my level as far as lyricism and street hip-hop. I just want people to know and understand the artistry and respect the type of music that I make. I think everybody makes different types of music and it's cool, but I'm here to show you that what it is that I do, this is timeless. I want people to really understand that I am [part] of the culture."

By knowing how to draw inspiration from and champion newness, while never compromising his own strengths, Pusha T has achieved a singular rap career in which his work stands the test of time while retaining its freshness. "I really feel like I'm making my mark. I'm part of a genre that is probably the youngest genre of music, and it was questioned so rough and now it's here to stay," he explained. "Success looks like longevity and being able to provide, being able to be a chameleon and change with the times. To be relevant in so many different times without compromising yourself."

Being a chameleon allows us to immerse ourselves in the creativity around us. It allows us to be energized and inspired by new ideas, and to understand the context that we're working in. If we can channel that energy into our own world, rather than imitating or chasing trends, then we can find new perspectives on our uncompromised vision.

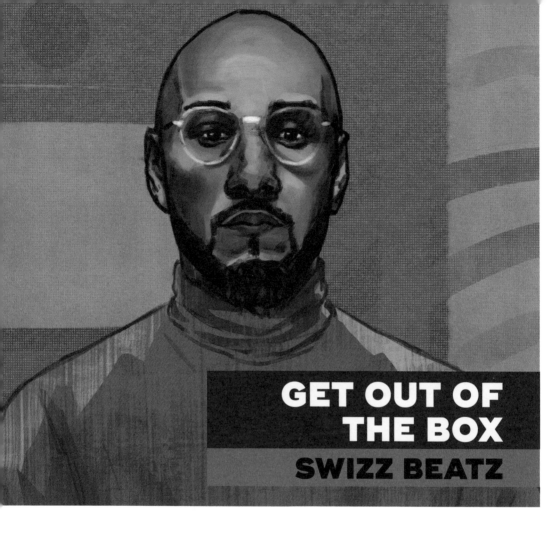

GET OUT OF THE BOX
SWIZZ BEATZ

A lot of skills and interests are transferable, and in a creative world that's constantly and quickly adapting, it's important that we're able to be reactive. In order to make the most out of our experience we need to look beyond what is immediately available to us, and welcome the opportunity to learn new things. We need to challenge ourselves by moving away from our comfort zones.

Swizz Beatz has never been afraid of thinking outside the box. As well as being a veteran record producer, Swizz has transcended beatmaking to become a champion for hip-hop culture in other spaces, including art, business, and tech. In response to the COVID-19 pandemic, he and Timbaland created the incredibly successful Verzuz platform—which showcases iconic artists going head to head in a celebration of their respective discographies—as a way of bringing global music fans together while they were stuck in their homes.

One afternoon in 2016, ahead of his "No Commission" art fair in London—an initiative that empowers artists by allowing them to retain all of the proceeds—he told me about the importance of exploring other disciplines in order to find better systems and approaches to enhance your own practice. "I just always thought globally. I always traveled," he explained. "I always was intrigued about being outside my box." Swizz recalled seeing the popularity of cellphones in Japan before they became a global phenomenon, and says he was met with doubt when he suggested to people back in the US that soon everybody would have one. "I seen all this stuff before it happened," he said. "I encourage people to step out of the box."

Swizz wasn't surprised when, upon being accepted to Harvard Business School's Owner/President Management Extension Program, people wondered why he'd need to attend. "People were like 'Oh, you're successful. Why are you going back to school?'" he remembered. But his response was simple: "If you're not a student of life, you're probably wasting life. You should always be open to get more knowledgeable in something that you're doing."

Swizz believes that for us to get the most out of life, we must be receptive to learning. By educating ourselves, we can access opportunities that otherwise might not have been available to us. When his interests became successful business ventures, Swizz decided he needed to learn the language of business. "I was like, 'Shit, they're still looking at me like I'm on-stage with DMX, even though I'm bringing these deals to the table,'" he said, reflecting on early boardroom experiences. "I didn't feel comfortable with it but I understood that I needed to go to the next level in my education to learn the language. I didn't have the language. Now we can talk about anything."

We can learn to sit with discomfort by continually challenging ourselves. By doing this regularly our comfort zone begins to expand, and what was previously outside the box will sit within. This will happen when we expand our knowledge and gather the information that we will need to navigate new spaces. Broadening our horizons helps us to become more rounded people: open to the opportunities that present themselves and able to apply skills across a broader range of practices.

STAY CURIOUS

PHARRELL WILLIAMS

To evolve and grow, it's paramount that we retain our curiosity. As children we are inherently interested in exploring the world around us—we ask questions about anything and everything. We are filled with wonder. But as we move toward adulthood many of us begin to feel like we know the answers, start to filter the information we gather based on how useful or practical it is, and lose that spirit of inquiry.

Pharrell Williams has built a decades-spanning career that has traversed multiple industries and inspired generations, by remaining inquisitive. "I'm just curious as an artist," he told me in 2019. "I really love finding new sounds, new textures, new chord progressions, a new way to communicate in a song... Not just being so textbook about things."

Despite everything that he has already achieved in his storied career, Pharrell hasn't become complacent, as he continues to explore new frontiers. "We can't necessarily determine what makes you relevant," he admitted. "But I know that reinvention is just that: something's different, something's new, something's evolved. Good, bad, or indifferent. I think that's where my mind is at all the time. I just want to know what else is there."

Driven by this thirst for knowledge, understanding, and perhaps most of all, feeling, Pharrell is guided by his student mentality. In fact, he told me you'd never catch him referring to himself as a "master." He learns from whatever presents itself to him, asking questions and listening as he walks through life, allowing curiosity to take the lead.

"I'm like this old cartoon called *Mr. Magoo*; he's like this short old man that just kind of keeps on walking, and it's not really clear as to whether he's blind or he just has his eyes closed," he explained. "But he walks into all kinds of things that should be calamitous, but nothing ever happens to him because he just uses his instincts to keep going. That's who I am. I often don't know where I'm going."

When there's a glimmer of curiosity in our minds, rather than interrogating its practicality, we can trust that it is worth following. Whether or not we can see where it will lead us in the moment, something within us was motivated to pick up that loose thread and follow the mystery. The satisfaction that comes from solving that is justification enough. Ask questions, listen carefully to the answers, read, and investigate. We must humble ourselves and remember that to be human is to be curious.

ABOUT THE
AUTHOR
GRANT BRYDON

Grant Brydon is a London-based writer whose work explores the intersection of hip-hop and mental health. During his decade-long career as a journalist, he has interviewed some of the world's biggest hip-hop artists. He also hosts the podcast *Making Conversation with Grant Brydon*. Brydon's work focuses on creativity, self-help and mental wellbeing. His writing has been published by *Highsnobiety*, *Clash*, *Esquire*, *Vice*, and many more.

ABOUT THE ILLUSTRATOR
KETU

Ketu is an LA-based artist, illustrator, and musician. He has worked with brands all over the world, including Universal Music Group, Pretty Bird, Facebook, Adobe, ACLU SoCal, NFL, and Netflix.

MENTAL HEALTH RESOURCES

If you feel affected by any of the issues discussed in this book, here is a non-exhaustive list of resources that offer support and information.

Global resources
Checkpoint: www.checkpointorg.com/global

Headspace: www.headspace.com

Rethink: www.rethink.org

United for Global Mental Health:
www.unitedgmh.org

North America
Active Minds: www.activeminds.org

Canadian Mental Health Association:
www.cmha.ca

Mental Health America:
www.mhanational.org

The Trevor Project: www.thetrevorproject.org

Youth Mental Health Canada:
www.ymhc.ngo

United Kingdom
Campaign Against Living Miserably (CALM): www.thecalmzone.net

Help Musicians: www.helpmusicians.org.uk

Hub of Hope: www.hubofhope.co.uk

Mind: www.mind.org.uk

Samaritans: www.samaritans.org

SANE: www.sane.org.uk

Spark and Co: www.sparkandco.co.uk

Australia and New Zealand:
Beyond Blue: www.beyondblue.org.au

ReachOut: au.reachout.com

R U OK?: www.ruok.org.au

SANE Australia: www.sane.org

I've been thinking about this book for almost a decade now, and have discussed it at various stages with so many amazing people. Each one of them has made a huge contribution, and without their input it wouldn't be in your hands right now. There are too many to name here, but I'll forever appreciate them all.

Thank you to Pete, Flo, and all of the team at DK for believing in the concept and publishing this book. To my editor, Mireille, for keeping my anxieties at bay and answering all of my questions about how this process works. To Oscar, my agent, for guiding me into publishing and sharing invaluable wisdom along the way. To Anthony for working tirelessly on illustrating each lesson and bringing these pages to life. To Brandon for the thoughtful foreword, and Vicky for the photograph.

To all of the artists and people that I have interviewed throughout my career, I have learned so much from you all and appreciate every word that has been shared with me over the years. Also to Frank, Scott, Shawn, Kendrick and Ye—we've never met, but you have all made a profound impact on me nonetheless.

To my family and friends for your patience and support throughout my life and career. And my wife Sophie, who—when I thought my dream of publishing this book would never happen—believed in me and encouraged me to keep going.

INDEX

Editors Mireille Harper and Florence Ward
Senior Designer Lauren Adams
Designer Lisa Sodeau
Senior Production Editor Marc Staples
Senior Production Controller Louise Minihane
Managing Editor Pete Jorgensen
Managing Art Editor Jo Connor
Publishing Director Mark Searle

DK would like to thank the author Grant Brydon, the illustrator Ketu,
Caroline West for proofreading and Julia March for index creation.
Photograph of Grant by Vicky Grout. Photograph of Ketu by Hadas.

First American Edition, 2022
Published in the United States by DK Publishing
1745 Broadway, 20th Floor, New York, NY 10019

A catalog record for this book is available from the Library of Congress.
ISBN: 978-0-7440-6119-2

DK books are available at special discounts when purchased in bulk for sales promotions, premiums,
fund-raising, or educational use. For details, contact:
DK Publishing Special Markets, 1745 Broadway, 20th Floor, New York, NY 10019
SpecialSales@dk.com

Printed and bound in Slovakia

For the curious
www.dk.com

This book was made with
Forest Stewardship Council™
certified paper—one small
step in DK's commitment
to a sustainable future.